The Vermont Nature Guide

Written and Illustrated

by

Sheri Amsel

Pinto Press

Cover design and illustration by Sheri Amsel

Publisher's Cataloging-in-Pubication
(provided by Quality Books, Inc.)

Amsel, Sheri
        The Vermont nature guide / written and illustrated by Sheri
        Amsel -- 1st ed.
        p. cm.
        Includes index.
        Preassigned LCCN: 98-65510
        ISBN: 0-9632476-7-0

        1. Natural history--Vermont. 2. Nature study--Vermont. 3.
        Vermont. I. Title.

QH105.V7A67 1998   508.743
                                QBI98-388

        10 9 8 7 6 5 4 3 2 1

Pinto Press

For
Marcia Perry, Sarah McKee,
Martha Broad & Joan Shulman...
remembering how those years in Vermont
shaped our lives forever.

Acknowledgments

I am grateful for the help I received from many sources: Maryke Gillis and the folks at The Nature Conservancy of Vermont for some of the "best" places to go, Jim Andrews at Middlebury College for his reptilian list, and especially Bob Popp at the Vermont Nongame and Natural Heritage Program for the difficult task of narrowing down the "most common" wildflowers that a book of this nature requires.

I also wish to thank Peter Osterhoudt who sat around the fire with us when we were kids dreaming up new adventures and making wilderness a passion, all while feeding us "river bottom stew."

Vermont

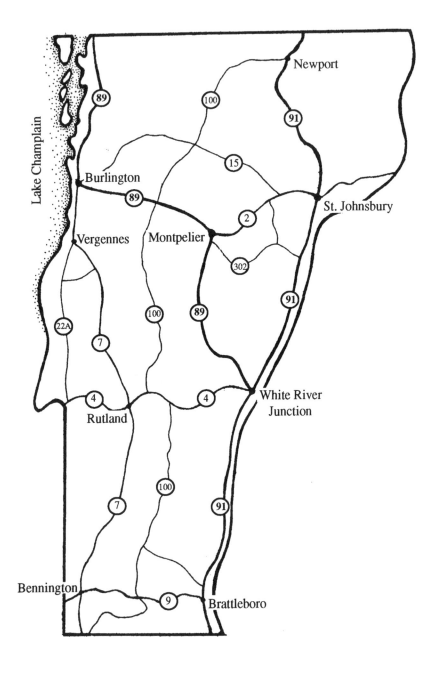

Table of Contents

Where to go..................................7
Birds......................................10
Wildflowers................................40
Mammals....................................60
Insects....................................76
Amphibians.................................92
Reptiles...................................96
Trees.....................................100
Species List and Index....................114

Vermont

Vermont encompasses many habitats in which to explore wild-life. Green rolling pastures, open woodlands, wetlands, and steep mountain tundra all contain a variety of wild species to discover. A relatively small state of only 9,615 square miles, Vermont has maintained its rural character. Even with the influx of many new residents seeking its special character, Vermont has remained a haven for wildlife and wild places.

In addition to more well-known hiking areas, like the Long Trail and the Green Mountain National Forest, there are countless places to observe wildlife. Several have been included in the following pages to get you started.

The *Vermont Nature Guide* contains some of the **most common** plant and animal life found in Vermont, with 83 birds, 52 wild-flowers, 36 mammals, 40 insects, 20 reptiles and amphibians and 33 trees. For easy identification, the description of each species is directly opposite the illustration. A check-off box is located in the back of the book for those keeping track of the species they have identified in the wild.

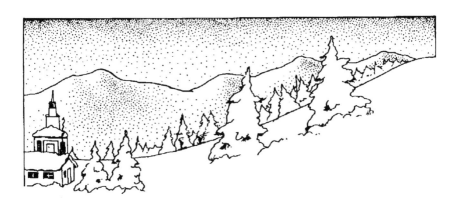

Where to Go...

The following areas are just a few of the places to
visit for identifying plants and animals.

1. Brighton State Park

Located south of the town of Island Pond off Rt. 105. In the summer the ranger
station supplies maps to many hiking trails and camping areas. Trails offer views
of boreal forest hardwood and softwood trees, birds, wildflowers and possibly
moose. For more information contact: Brighton State Park, Island Pond, VT
05846 at (802) 723-4360 (summer) and (802) 479-4280 (winter).

2. Maidstone State Park

Located 5 miles south of Broomfield off Rt. 102. Look for signs on the right for
the entrance and travel another 5 miles down the dirt road to the ranger station.
Trails travel through woodlands and lakeside where hikers can spot birds and
wildflowers. For more information about camping contact: Maidstone State
Park, RFD 1, Box 455, Guildhall, VT
05905 at (802) 676-3930.

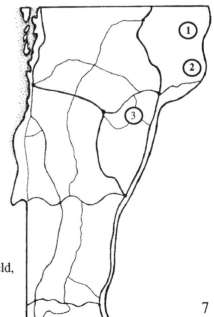

3. Groton State Forest

Located south of Rt. 2 between Barre
and St. Johnsbury off Rt. 232. This
park contains many trails and a nature
center. Hikers can visit a bog, travel
through hardwood forest and view
many species of trees, birds and
wildflowers. For more information
contact: Groton State Forest, Marshfield,
Vt. 05658 at (802) 584-3820.

7

4. The "East Woods"

Located just south of Burlington where Rt. 7 meets I-89, identified by a small parking area and sign. The trail passes huge maples, pines and hemlocks and hikers may identify many tree species, wild plants and birds. For more information contact: The University of Vermont Natural Areas Environment Program, The Bittersweet, 153 S. Prospect Street, Burlington, VT 05405 at (802) 656-4055.

5. Green Mountain Audubon Center

Located south of Richmond (exit 11 off I-89). Travel toward Huntington about five miles to Sherman Hollow Rd. on the right to the Nature Center. A variety of trails travel through woodlands for viewing trees, wild plants and birds. For more information contact: The Green Mountain Audubon Center, RD 1, Box 189, Richmond, VT 05477 at (802) 434-3068.

6. Branbury State Park

Located east of Rt. 7 on Rt 53. A trail beginning at the sign for the Falls of Lana will take hikers up to Silver Lake, around which an interpretive trail passes many species of trees, wild plants and birds. For more information contact: Branbury State Park, RFD 2, Box 2421, Brandon, VT 05733 at (802) 247-5925.

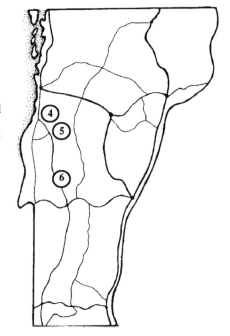

8

The following nature preserves are either owned or maintained by The Nature Conservancy of Vermont. For more information or specific directions call: The Nature Conservancy of Vermont, (802) 229-4425.

7. Shaw Mountain Natural Area

Entering Benson from 22A go through four corners and travel one mile to take the first left onto gravel road. Then take next right ($^3/_4$ mile) and go 1.5 miles to Shaw Mountain Natural Area sign on the left. The trail leads hikers through a oak and hickory forest with a variety of plant life, rare and common. Among the wildlife are wild turkeys and spotted salamanders, which breed in the area.

8. Chickering Bog Natural Area

North of Montpelier take Rt. 2 to E. Montpelier onto Rt. 14. Then travel past N. Montpelier 1.1 miles to Lightning Ridge Rd on left. Drive 1.6 miles and park along the road across from the TNC green post marking entrance. The trail passes through forest and bog for viewing wetland plants, northern cedar, tamarack, white pine and an actual quaking bog. Hikers are cautioned to stay on the trail. Wet feet and bugs are likely.

9. Barr Hill Nature Preserve

Located north of Hardwick off Rt. 16. Travel to the town of Greensboro and continue north out of town turning right at the Town Hall and then left at the first fork. Then go to the closed gate at the George Hill Farm. Open (and close) the gate to proceed to the preserve parking area. The trails are less than a mile and have informational stations that tell about the natural history of the area.

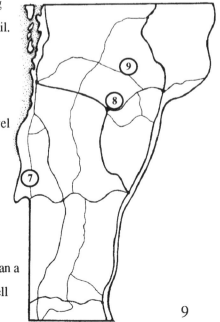

Vermont Birds

Vermont is home to a huge number of birds, many more than are contained on these pages. A large portion of these birds arrive from winter territory to breed in the north in the warmer months. Many birds overwinter in Vermont. Some birds pass through in the spring to summer farther north and may just appear briefly at feeders in mid-April. These short-term visitors may not be included in this text.

It is easier to see the markings and colors that help to identify a bird if you can look at it with binoculars. However, as you get to know the markings to look for, and become familiar with the birds in Vermont, it will be easier to name them from a distance. To see more birds, move slowly and quietly and wear dull-colored clothes. Birds do see color.

The pictures you see in this section are of adult male birds in breeding plumage. Females are duller in color, which helps protect them while nesting, and are more difficult to identify.

Body measurements given are from the beak to the tip of the tail. Arrows point to specific characteristics that distinguish one species from another.

The illustration opposite shows the correct names of a bird's body parts. This will help you to identify a bird by locating markings correctly.

Body length from beak to end of tail.

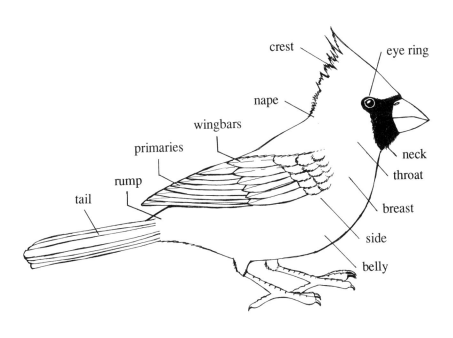

crest

eye ring

nape

wingbars

primaries

rump

tail

neck

throat

breast

side

belly

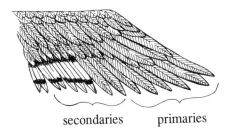

secondaries   primaries

Birds of the forest and field:

Ruffed Grouse
Located in mixed forests, along roadways. Winters in coniferous areas. Large bird, dark, gray-brown dappling above, lighter below. Fan-shaped, barred tail. "Drums" in the spring for a mate. Feeds on buds. Usually spotted on ground then bursts into flight when alarmed. **Spruce Grouse** - Located in coniferous forests. Rare. Has black throat and red eyebrow.

Wild Turkey
Located in open woodlands and clearings. Often seen along roadways. Looks similar to domestic turkey except slimmer with rusty-brown tail feathers instead of white. Eats fruits, seeds and acorns. Travels in flocks, roosting in trees and running when startled. Weak fliers.

Whippoorwill
Located in open woodlands near fields. Mottled brown bird with small beak and large mouth, flat head, black throat and white neck band. Feeds on moths and other insects caught in flight. Strictly nocturnal, calling at dusk. In daylight blends into the forest floor.

Nighthawk
Located in woodlands near open fields. Mottled brown like whippoorwill but with white throat and wing stripe. Long pointed wings are especially visible at dusk when they circle above and dive after insects.

Crow
Located in woodlands, fields and residential areas. All black. Flaps wings in flight instead of gliding like hawks. Feeds as a scavenger. Distinctive *caw* call.

12

Ruffed
Grouse
14 - 19"

Spruce
Grouse
15 - 17"

Wild Turkey
34 - 48 "

whippoorwill
9 - 10"

Crow
17 - 21"

Nighthawk
9 - 10"

13

Birds commonly found in wetter areas:

Common Loon

Located on lakes and rivers seasonally. Large bird with dark head and white chest. Dark back with dapples of white. Rides low in the water. Comes ashore only to breed and nest. Yodel-like call often heard at night. Dives for fish.

Osprey

Located along rivers, ponds and lakes. Dark above and white below. White head with dark line across side of face. Wings have distinctive crook in the middle visible in flight. Dives for fish, which it catches in its talons. Often submerges completely when diving for fish.

Common Merganser

Located on streams, rivers, lakes and ponds. Dark green head. Distinctive white breast and sides. Long, thin, red bill, serrated on both sides. Female, most commonly seen with hatchlings on the water, has more of a crest on its rust-colored head. Swims in small flocks. Often seen facing upstream, fishing.

Canada Goose

Located by rivers, lakes, streams and in marshes. Huge bird with brownish body, long black neck and head and distinctive white cheek patch. Feeds on plants (and grain). Gathers in large flocks to fly in the distinctive V, punctuated with honking calls.

American Bittern

Located in marshy wetlands. Very shy. Mottled, brown heron with distinctive black cheek streak. Hides in tall vegetation standing with head pointed upward. Active at night. Solitary. Feeds mostly on fish.

Common Loon
28 - 36"

Osprey
21 - 24"

Common Merganser
22 - 27"

American Bittern
23 - 34"

Canada Goose
25 - 35"

15

Belted Kingfisher

Located by rivers, ponds and lakes. Long sharp bill. Bushy head crest. Gray-blue head, back and wings. White chin and belly with dark band across breast. Hovers over water to dive for fish. Loud rattling call.

Red-winged Blackbird

Located in marshy areas, grassy fields and pastures. Black body with bright red patch on the shoulder. Travels in large groups, eating seeds, grains, insects. Distinctive, loud call.

Wood Duck

Located along wooded rivers, ponds and swamps. Multi-colored duck with red bill, distinctive head crest and white chin patch. Will nest in tree cavities and man-made nesting boxes. Eats plants and some insects.

Blue-winged Teal

Located on ponds, lakes and marshes. A small brown duck with distinctive white crescent in front of the eye. Also blue shoulder patches and green on inner wing feathers (speculum). Flies rapidly. Often in small flocks.

Mallard

Located in fresh water ponds, marshes, lakes and water-filled ditches. Green head with white neck ring and rust-colored chest. Blue speculum. Females mottled. Feeds on water plants and leftover grain in farm fields.

Great Blue Heron

Located in marshes, by rivers, lakes and ponds. Tall, gray stork-like body and whitish head. Flies with crooked neck, 7 ft. wing span. Can be spotted standing statue-like by water's edge. Feeds mainly on fish.

Belted Kingfisher 12 - 13"

Wood Duck 17 - 20"

Red-winged Blackbird 7 - 9"

Blue-winged Teal 15 -16"

Great Blue Heron 38 - 52"

Mallard 20 - 27"

The perching birds:

Evening Grosbeak

Located mostly in coniferous forests. Large yellow body with dark head and white wing patches. Huge pale beak and yellow eyebrow. Seed eater. Winters in flocks, commonly at seed feeders.

Rose-breasted Grosbeak

Located in deciduous woods, orchards, yards. Large bird with black back, white belly and red chest patch. Female mottled brown and white. Large beak. Feeds on insects, seeds and buds. Visits feeders.

Red Crossbill

Located in coniferous forests. Brick-red body with dark wings. Bill crossed at the tip. Females are dull-colored with yellow rump patch. Feeds on conifer seeds. Travels in flocks appearing sporadically all winter.

Purple Finch

Located in forests, gardens and at house feeders. Rosy head, chest and rump. May travel in flocks, sings loudly and feeds at feeders all winter.

Cardinal

Located in thickets, woodland edges, suburban gardens and feeders. Bright red bird with head crest and cone-shaped beak. Feeds on seeds and insects. Visits feeders all winter. Aggressive and territorial.

Common Redpoll

Located in scrubby fields. Mottled brown with red crown, black chin patch and rosy areas on breast and rump. Feeds on seeds. Comes to feeders.

Evening
Grosbeak
7 - 8"

Rose-breasted
Grosbeak
8"

Red Crossbill
5 - 6"

Purple Finch
5 - 6"

Cardinal
8 - 9"

Common Redpoll
5"

19

Goldfinch

Located in fields, bushes and bordering trees. Bright yellow with white rump patch and black forehead, wings and tail. Travels in flocks, feeding on seeds and insects. Females and winter males duller in color.

Pine Sisken

Located in coniferous forests, thickets and shrubby fields. Mottled brown streaks all over with yellow at base of tail and on wings. Thin, sharp beak and notched tail. Feeds on seeds, visiting feeders all winter.

Common Yellowthroat

Located in open and shrubby fields. Brown on top with distinctive black eye patch and yellow throat and breast. Usually found on or near the ground.

American Redstart

Located in deciduous forests and thickets. Black with sandy, orange wing and tail patches. Females are brown with yellow patches. Feeds on insects caught in flight.

Swallows

Several kinds found nesting in areas described by their names. Long, pointed wings and notched tails. All are strong fliers snatching insects in mid-flight. Barn swallows are blue above and rusty below with long, forked tails. Tree swallows have green backs and white bellies. Purple martins (7 - 8") are dark all over with shiny, purple backs, heads, tops of wings.

Eastern Bluebird

Located in open woodlands, fields, farms. Bright blue above with reddish breast and white belly. Will sit up on a high perch to hunt for insects. Arrives with spring.

Goldfinch
4 - 5"

Pine Sisken
4 - 5"

Common Yellowthroat
4 - 5 "

American Redstart
4 - 5"

Barn Swallow
5 - 6"

Eastern Bluebird
7"

Purple Martin

Tree Swallow

Barn Swallow

Bobolink

Located in open fields, flocking near marsh lands. Black front, wings and tail with white rump and wing patches. Sandy yellow patch on back of head. Lighter on top than underneath. Short, cone-shaped bill.

Meadowlark

Located in fields and pastures. Robin-sized with brown streaked back, yellow throat and belly and black V on chest. White outer tail feathers. Often found singing loudly on fence posts or wires.

Northern Oriole

Found in deciduous forest and shade trees. Black head, back, wings and tail. Orange breast, rump and shoulder patch. Female is brown with yellow underneath. May travel in flocks.

Rufous-sided Towhee

Located in brushy areas and along the edge of woods. Black head and top of body. White belly with rust-colored flanks. Ground feeders, scratching for seeds and insects in the leaves.

Cedar Waxwing

Located in open woodlands, orchards and yards. Olive-brown with a distinct head crest, black mask, and yellow tips on the ends of the tail feathers. Red tips on the wing feathers. Travels in flocks eating berries.

Horned Lark

Located in sparse, open fields. Brownish bird with black dash under eye and black chest patch. Black "horns" on head often indistinct. Searches on the ground for insects and seeds.

Bobolink
6 - 8"

Meadowlark
9 - 11"

Northern
Oriole
7 - 8"

Rufous-sided
Towhee
7 - 9"

Cedar
Waxwing
6 - 8"

Horned Lark
6 - 8"

23

White-breasted Nuthatch

Located in deciduous forests. Small bird with black cap, gray-blue back and wings. White face, breast and belly. Creeps down trees headfirst after insects and seeds. Common at bird feeders throughout winter.

Red-breasted Nuthatch

Located in coniferous forest. Small bird with black cap, gray-blue back and wings. Rust-colored breast and belly. Black line through eye from beak. Eats conifer seeds and small insects while creeping down trees headfirst. Seen all winter. Will come to feeders.

Ruby-throated Hummingbird

Located in woods, gardens. Tiny bird; metallic green above, pale below with bright red throat. Long, slender bill. Often hovers near tubular flowers collecting nectar. Attracted to red blossoms. Drinks at feeders.

Tufted Titmouse

Located in moist woodlands. Gray above, white below. Rusty flanks. Crest on head. Feeds on insects and seeds. Overwinters. Visits feeders.

Golden-crowned Kinglet

Located mostly in conifer forests but also found in mixed woodlands and thickets. Tiny bird with olive back, wings and tail. Light colored below. White eyebrow and ruby crown with yellow border then black border. Females have all-yellow crown. Insect eater. Present all winter.

Ruby-crowned Kinglet

Located in conifer forests, mixed woodlands and thickets. Tiny bird; olive-green above, light-colored below. White eye ring. Ruby crown only visible when bird is agitated. Sings loudly. Flicks wings.

White-breasted
Nuthatch
5"

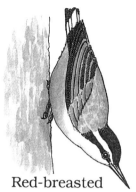

Red-breasted
– Nuthatch
4"

Ruby-throated
Hummingbird
3 - 4"

Tufted
Titmouse
5 - 6"

Golden-crowned
Kinglet
3 - 4"

Ruby-crowned
Kinglet
3 - 4"

Pileated Woodpecker

Located in dense deciduous forests and mixed woods. Large crow-sized bird. Mostly black with white stripes down face and neck and conspicuous red head crest. Wary, taps trees for insects. Loud ringing call and strong flight.

Hairy Woodpecker

Located in deciduous forests and mixed woods. About robin-sized with white back, black and white barred wings and red patch on head. Long, slender bill. Pecks for insects in trees.

Downy Woodpecker Identical to hairy except distinctly smaller. Smallest woodpecker with smaller bill.

Northern Flicker (Yellow-shafted Flicker)

Located in open areas with trees. Large, brown woodpecker with dark bars on back and spotted lighter belly. Black neck, cheek patch. Red on the back of head, yellow wing tips. Searches ground for insects.

Red-headed Woodpecker

Located in open woods, farms, orchards. Mid-sized woodpecker with completely red head. Black back, wings and tail. Distinctive white wing and rump patches. Prefers dead standing trees. Catches insects in flight.

Yellow-bellied Sapsucker

Located in open woods, orchards and gardens. Brown mottled back with lighter front. Red crown. Red chin bordered by black. Distinctive white, vertical stripe on wings. Common but shy. Taps trees for sap and insects. Mewing call.

Blue Jay

Located in oak forests and suburbs. Head crest. Bright blue above with black bars. White below. Feeds on nuts, seeds. Loud call. Aggressive.

Pileated Woodpecker
16 - 19$\frac{1}{2}$"

Hairy
Woodpecker
8 - 9"

Red-
headed
Woodpecker
8 -10"

Yellow-
bellied
Sapsucker
7 - 8"

Northern Flicker
(Yellow-shafted Flicker)
10 - 12"

Blue Jay
10 - 12"

27

Dark-eyed Junco (Slate-colored Junco)

Located in coniferous forests, mixed forests, fields and thickets. Slate gray all over except for white belly and along edges of tail. Seed eater. Very common at feeders all winter.

Chickadee

Located in mixed forests, open woodlands and suburban areas. Black cap and throat with white cheeks. Gray back, wings and tail. White belly. Feeds on insects and seeds. Common at feeders all winter. *Chick-a-dee-dee-dee* call.

House Sparrow

Located all over from farms to towns. Black bill, chin and chest with white cheeks and brown patch behind eyes. May travel in flocks. Common at house feeders.

White-throated Sparrow

Located in forest undergrowth and brush often in coniferous forests. Black and white striped head with distinct white throat. Feeds on seeds, often on the ground. Often in flocks. Can be seen all winter.

House Wren

Located in brush and shrubbery. Small brown bird, darker on top, lighter below. Often stands with narrow, rounded tail cocked. Long, slim bill. Feeds on insects. Aggressively territorial.

Fox Sparrow

Located in coniferous forest undergrowth. Also in mixed woods, fields and thickets. The largest sparrow. Rusty brown above with same color mottling below. Dark breast spot. Scratches on ground for food.

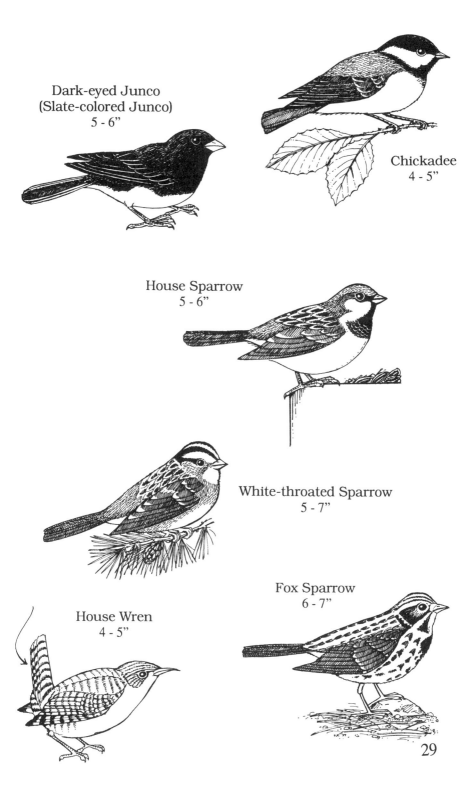

Dark-eyed Junco
(Slate-colored Junco)
5 - 6"

Chickadee
4 - 5"

House Sparrow
5 - 6"

White-throated Sparrow
5 - 7"

Fox Sparrow
6 - 7"

House Wren
4 - 5"

29

Eastern Wood Pewee

Located in mixed woods, orchards and parks. Grayish bird overall. Head not darker like a phoebe and lower mandible of beak lighter. Prominent white wing bars. Notched tail. No eye ring. Longer wings than phoebe. Rarely wags tail.

Eastern Phoebe

Located in open woodlands near water. Prefers cliffs, bridges and buildings. Olive-gray, darker head than back, solid black bill, no wing bars or eye ring. Catches insects in flight. Wags tail. *Phoe-be* call.

Great Crested Flycatcher

Located in deciduous and mixed woods. Olive head and back with long rusty-brown tail. Yellowish belly. Large head and bill adapted for catching insects.

Olive-sided Flycatcher

Located in moist coniferous forests and bogs. Olive-brown on top with dark flanks, white down center of breast. White tufts under wings. Large head and bill. Perches on dead snags for fly catching.

Red-eyed Vireo

Located in deciduous forests and suburban areas with big shade trees. Gray head, olive on top, whitish below. Distinct white eyebrow bordered by black. Red eyes. Feeds on insects. Strong singer.

Eastern Kingbird

Located in open fields, farms and roadsides. Often spotted on fence posts and wires. Dark above with black head. White below. White tail tips. Catches insects on the wing. Aggressive. Calls loudly.

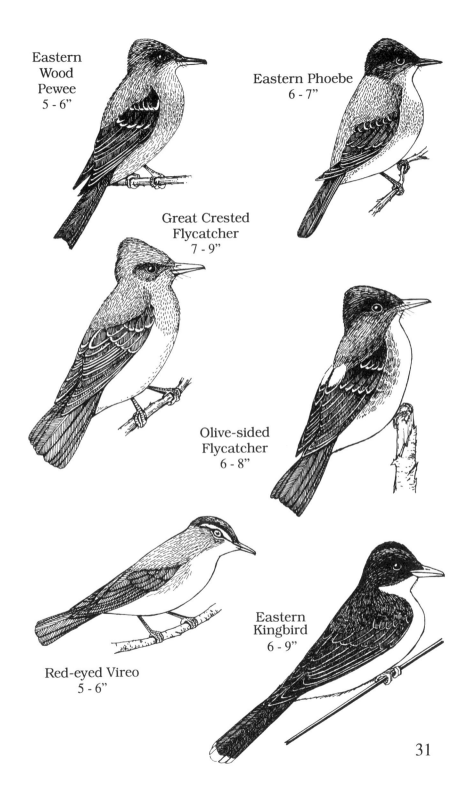

Eastern
Wood
Pewee
5 - 6"

Eastern Phoebe
6 - 7"

Great Crested
Flycatcher
7 - 9"

Olive-sided
Flycatcher
6 - 8"

Red-eyed Vireo
5 - 6"

Eastern
Kingbird
6 - 9"

31

Veery

Located in deciduous forests. Smaller than a robin. Rusty-brown above, lighter below with rusty spotting on breast. Eats insects on the ground and fruits. Strong singer.

American Robin

Located in open woodlands, farms, fields, towns. Gray above with darker head and tail. Rusty-orange below. Eats worms and insects.

Hermit Thrush

Located in moist woodland areas. Olive-brown back with a rusty-brown tail. Lighter below with dark spotting on breast. Raises its tail repeatedly. Eats insects and berries. May overwinter. Strong flute-like song.

Wood Thrush

Located in deciduous forests with thick, brushy undergrowth. Brown with rusty head. White below with dark, round spots on breast and belly. Eats insects and berries. Sings a fluting *pit-pit-pit*.

Catbird

Located in thickets in dense cover. Dark gray all over with distinct black cap and rusty-brown under tail. Flicks its long tail. Known for its cat-like mewing call.

Brown Thrasher

Located in thickets and scrubby fields. Rust-brown above, striped below. Longer tail, lighter colored eyes than wood thrush. Long slender bill. Strong singer.

American Robin
9 - 11"

Veery
6 - 7"

Wood Thrush
7 - 8"

Hermit Thrush
6 - 8"

Catbird
8 - 9"

Brown
Thrasher
10 - 11"

33

Brown-headed Cowbird

Located in farmland, fields and golf courses. Overall dark bird with brown head down to shoulders and rest of body black. Travels in flocks. Females lay eggs in other birds' nests to be raised by other females (parasitic).

Common Grackle

Located in open fields and farmland. Large, dark bird with iridescent head. Long tail that widens at the end. Long thin beak. Flocks to feed on the ground with other species of birds.

American Woodcock

Located in moist woodlands and thickets near open fields. Rounded, stocky bird with long, thin bill and short neck. Distinctive dark bars across head. Blends in, hard to spot. Eats mostly worms. Active at dusk. Courtship display - aerial spirals with plunging dives and calls.

Mourning Dove

Located in fields, farmland, residential areas and parks. Tan-colored, slim body. Long, pointed tail with white border. Eats seeds and fruits. Cooo-coo-coo call.

Snipe

Located by ponds, in marshes, wet meadows and bogs. Brown and tan stripes run down head and back. Long, thin bill. Orange tail in flight. When flushed, flies quickly and erratically. Feeds in early morning and dusk.

Killdeer

Located in fields, pastures and golf courses. Brown above and white below with two black bands on the breast. Rusty top of tail. Pretends wing is broken when nest is approached.

Common Grackle
10 - 12"

Brown-headed Cowbird
6 - 7"

Mourning Dove
10 - 12"

American Woodcock
8 - 11"

Killdeer
8 - 11"

Snipe
9 - 11"

35

Woodland birds of prey:

Screech Owl

Found in wooded areas and orchards. Small and mottled, rusty-brown to gray with distinct "ears." Bravely defends nest. Eats wide variety of prey from rodents to insects. Call is wavering whistle or short notes.

Barred Owl

Found in wet, swampy, forested areas. Large grayish-brown owl with dark bars across the neck and breast and dark vertical bars on the belly. Dark eyes. Active at night, feeding on mice, birds and frogs. Call is usually 8 hoots.

Great Horned Owl

Located in all habitats from forested to open country. Large bird with widely spaced and distinct ear tufts. Barred belly and breast with white throat. Eats wide variety of prey from rabbits to beetles. Call is 4 - 7 low hoots.

Northern Saw-whet Owl

Located in moist coniferous forests. Small brown owl. White chest with rusty vertical stripes. No ear tufts. Nocturnal feeding on rodents. Call is long series of short whistles.

Sharp-shinned Hawk

Located in woodlands. Shorter wings. Long, narrow, barred tail. Pale belly and breast with rusty mottling. Preys on small birds, rodents and frogs. Commonly seen migrating in groups along treetops.

Broad-winged Hawk

Located mainly in deciduous woodlands. Rusty bars on breast and belly with a broad, black-and-white banded tail. Feeds on snakes, rodents, frogs and insects.

Screech Owl
10"

Barred Owl
19 - 20"

Great
Horned
Owl
23 - 25"

Northern
Saw-whet Owl
7"

Broad-winged
Hawk
13 - 15"

Sharp-shinned
Hawk
10 -14"

37

Open country birds of prey:

Red-tailed Hawk
Located in fields adjacent to woodlands. Large hawk with dark head and back, lighter below with a dark band across the belly and a rust tail. Very variable in color. Soars while hunting or sits high on a tree or pole to scan for prey. Feeds mostly on rodents.

Marsh Hawk
Located in grasslands and marshes. Slim bodied and pale underneath with prominent white rump patch. Glides low above ground with wings tipped up above horizontal plane. Hunts mostly for rodents.

Kestrel
Located in any open area, including towns and parks. Most common and smallest of the falcons. Rust-colored back and tail, dark patches on the face and long, pointed, gray-blue wings (females have rust wings). About the size of a blue jay. Hunts insects, small birds and mice by hovering over open areas or perching up high.

Northern Shrike
Located in open woodlands to fields. Uncommon but distinctive when spotted. Pale back, white breast and belly. Black face mask and hooked bill. Robin sized. Perches on fence posts and tree tops scanning for small birds, rodents and frogs. Impales prey on thorns or barbed wire.

Turkey Vulture
Located in open areas and along roadways. Dark overall with large wingspread and two-toned wing feathers underneath. Holds wings in V and circles high in sky. Scavenger and carrion eater.

Red-tailed Hawk
19 - 23"

Marsh Hawk
17 - 19"

Kestrel
9 - 12"

Northern Shrike
9 - 10"

Turkey Vulture
25 - 30"

Wildflowers

Many Vermont wildflowers have a short growing season that begins in late April and is often over by early July. Other wildflowers, however, persist throughout the summer at higher elevations (mountaintops) where it is cooler. Many Vermont wildflowers are considered endangered and are protected by law from being picked.

In this guide most of the wildflowers are soft-stemmed, usually flowering in the spring and growing into fruits or pods housing seeds in the summer and fall.

Blossoms, fruits and leaves can take many forms. These characteristics will help you identify the plants from their descriptions. The following illustrations should help clarify any of the terminology used in the wildflower section.

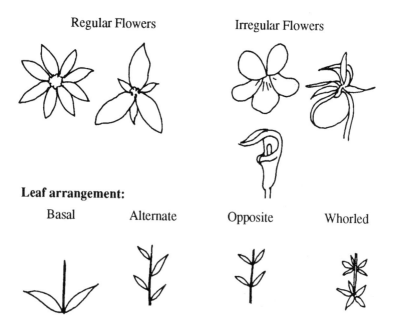

Regular Flowers   Irregular Flowers

Leaf arrangement:

Basal   Alternate   Opposite   Whorled

Leaves:

Simple   Palmately Compound   Pinnately Compound

Leaf Shapes:

Lance-shaped   Ovate   Oblong   Elliptical

Leaf Edges:

Entire   Toothed   Lobed

Flower Type:

Umbel   Spike   Raceme

Found in moist and dry woods:

Bunchberry (May - July)

White petal-like leaves surround small, **greenish** flower cluster. In summer the flower turns to a cluster of bright red berries. Ovate leaves come to a point, arranged in a whorl beneath flower. Found in cool woods, bogs.

Bluebead Lily or Yellow Clintonia (May - July)

Greenish yellow, nodding flowers. Flowers turn to a cluster of dark blue berries in summer. Leaves are long, wide, with pointed ends, pointing upward in a basal attachment. Found in moist woods.

Great Solomon's Seal (May - June)

Greenish flowers are small, 1/2 inch, hanging in clusters of 2 - 10 along arching stem. Flowers turn to dark berries in summer. Leaves are large, ribbed, pointed ellipses. Found in woods and river banks.

False Solomon's Seal (May - June)

Flowers are small, **white** and growing in clusters at the end of a long, arching stem. Flowers turn to red berries. Long, ribbed, elliptical leaves with pointed ends. Found in wooded areas.

Goldthread (May - early July)

Delicate, single, **white** flower on bare stem. Evergreen leaves have three leaflets and are on separate stem. Found in cool, moist woods, bogs.

Indian Pipe (June - Sept)

Waxy, **white** plant with nodding flower at top. May be pinkish. Lacking chlorophyll, this plant is a saprophyte living off decaying matter. Found in woodlands.

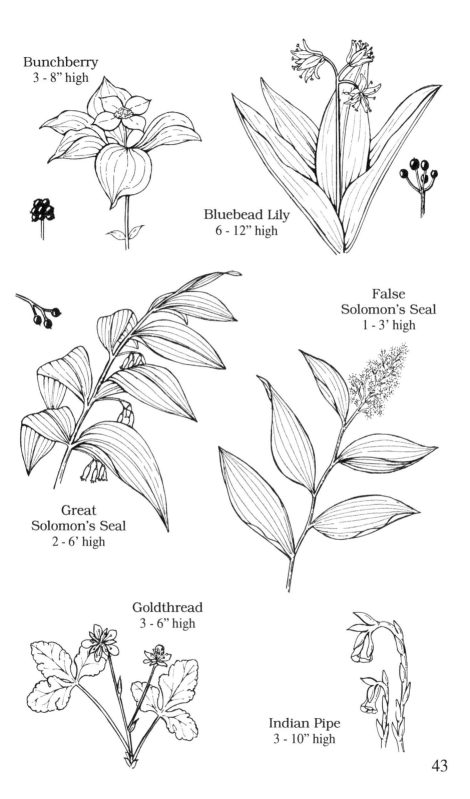

Bunchberry
3 - 8" high

Bluebead Lily
6 - 12" high

False
Solomon's Seal
1 - 3' high

Great
Solomon's Seal
2 - 6' high

Goldthread
3 - 6" high

Indian Pipe
3 - 10" high

43

Painted Trillium (April - June)

Three-petaled **white flower with scarlet veining** at the base of each petal. Three pointed, ovate leaves whirl around stem below flower. Found in cool, moist woods.

Red Trillium (April - June)

Three-petaled, **dark red-maroon** flower. Three pointed, ovate leaves whorl around stem below the flower. Flower has unpleasant odor. Found in wooded areas.

Pink Lady Slipper (May - early July)

Lone flower is **pink**, hollow pouch with darker pink veins. Bare stem with large, linear leaves attached basally. Found in bogs and moist woods especially in pine forests.

Spring Beauty (April - May)

Small, delicate **white to pink** flowers with pink veins and five petals. Each stem has a cluster of flowers and one pair of oval *or* long narrow leaves (leaf shapes represent two separate species). Found in moist woods.

Wild Ginger (April - June)

Dark, **reddish-brown**, cup-shaped flower with 3 pointed lobes growing at ground level in the junction between two hairy leaf stems. The two leaves are large (3 - 6"), heart-shaped and hairy. Found in the woods.

Common Wood Sorrel (May - July)

Small, **white to pink** flowers with pink veins and five petals. One flower per stalk. Clover-like leaves are basal with sour taste. Found in thick bunches growing in damp, shady wooded areas.

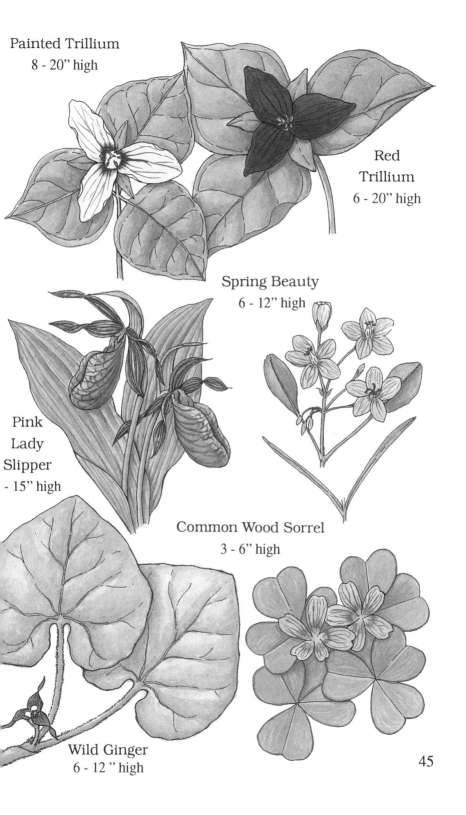

Painted Trillium
8 - 20" high

Red
Trillium
6 - 20" high

Spring Beauty
6 - 12" high

Pink
Lady
Slipper
- 15" high

Common Wood Sorrel
3 - 6" high

Wild Ginger
6 - 12 " high

45

Found in moist woods and wetlands:

Northern Pitcher Plant (June - July)

Nodding, **purplish-red** flower on a leafless stalk. Leaves are long, hollow "pitchers" that are green with purple veins. An insectivorous plant, its leaves contain downward-pointing hairs and fill with water to entrap insects. Found in sphagnum bogs.

Pickerelweed (June - October)

Spikes of small **violet-blue** flowers rise above the water. Large, heart-shaped leaves on long stalks attached basally. Found along edges of ponds, lakes, streams and marshes. Prefers calm water.

Blue Flag (May - July)

Showy **blue-violet** flowers with 3 petals and 3 yellow-veined sepals. One to several flowers sit on top of sturdy stem with tall sword-like leaves attaching basally. Found in marshes and wet meadows.

Jack-in-the-Pulpit (April - June)

Flower is a small spike inside a green and purple striped cup with drooping hood. Spike turns to cluster of red berries. Leaves have long stem and three large leaflets. Found in wet woods and swamps.

Marsh Blue Violet (April - June)

Purple irregular flower, darker toward the center with hairy side petals on tall leafless stalk. Heart-shaped leaves. Found in wet places.

Similar to **Common Blue Violet** except Common has a spur on the lower petal, distinct veins on petals and larger leaves. Found in yards.

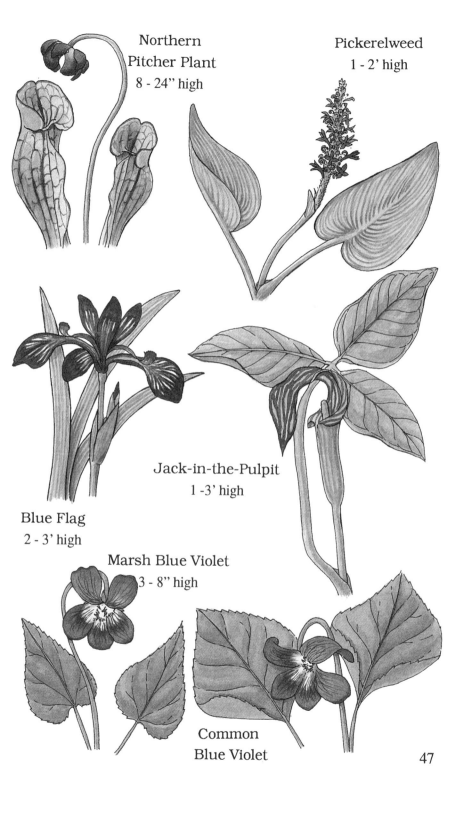

Northern
Pitcher Plant
8 - 24" high

Pickerelweed
1 - 2' high

Jack-in-the-Pulpit
1 -3' high

Blue Flag
2 - 3' high

Marsh Blue Violet
3 - 8" high

Common
Blue Violet

47

Found in fields, shores and roadsides:

Purple Loosestrife (June - September)
Purple-pink, wrinkled-petal flowers on tall, spiked stem above whorls of 2 - 3 long, thin leaves. Found in wet meadows often in large masses crowding out native plants. Introduced from Europe.

New England Aster (August - October)
Many **violet** flowers with yellow center discs clustered on top of a stout, branching, hairy stem. Leaves crowd the stem. They are long, thin, pointed and clasp the stem. Found in moist fields, along shorelines and swamps. Similar to smooth-stemmed New York Aster.

Chicory (June - October)
Showy **blue** flower with fringed petal tips. Flowers are stalkless and arranged around stiff stem. Leaves are 3 - 6" long arranged basally, smaller on stems. Leaves similar in shape to dandelion leaves. Found in fields and along roadsides.

Cow Vetch (May - August)
Small, **violet-blue**, tubular flowers clustered on one side of long stem. Pinnately compound leaves made up of 8 -12 small, pointed leaflets in opposite pattern on thin, delicate vine-like stem. Each leaf has pair of vine tendrils at end. Found in fields and roadsides.

Harebell (June - September)
Nodding, **violet-blue** flowers are bell-shaped, each on a delicate stem. Many long, narrow leaves on stem. Basal leaves are more heart-shaped and fade by bloom time. Found on rocky banks, fields and shorelines.

48

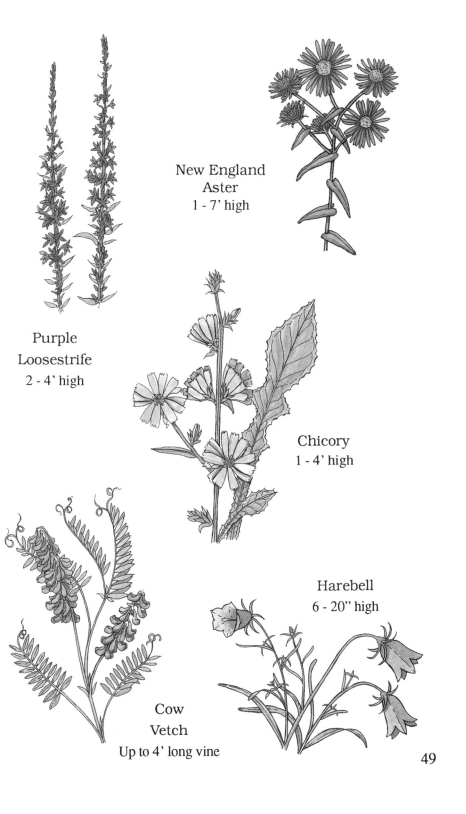

New England
Aster
1 - 7' high

Purple
Loosestrife
2 - 4' high

Chicory
1 - 4' high

Harebell
6 - 20" high

Cow
Vetch
Up to 4' long vine

49

Creeping Bellflower (June - August)

Nodding **blue** bells arranged in a line on one side of long stem. Leaves along lower stem are oval with toothed edges and pointed ends. Found in fields and on roadsides.

Blind Gentian (August - October)

Dark blue, tubular flowers sealed at the end and arranged in clusters at the top of stem and where upper leaves meet stem. Thin, pointed leaves are in whorls at the top of the stem and opposite toward the bottom. Found in moist fields, meadows and brushy areas.

Bluets (April - July)

Tiny, **pale blue**, tubular flowers with yellowish centers each growing on delicate stems. Small, oblong, basal leaves and some pairs on stem oppositely arranged. Found in large patches on grassy slopes and fields.

Blue-eyed Grass (June - July)

Tiny, dark, **violet-blue** flower with yellow center on grass-like stem. Found in fields and meadows.

Common Speedwell (May - August)

Tiny, **lavender** flowers clustered on long stalks that grow where leaves meet stem. Leaves are elliptical with rounded ends and toothed edges. Hairy stem. Found in fields, open woods, often in large masses trailing along ground.

Meadowsweet (June - September)

Cluster of **white to pale pink** small flowers at the top of a thick stem. Leaves are oval with toothed edges, pointed ends and lighter underneath. Tall, woody shrub. Found in fields, moist meadows and along roadsides.

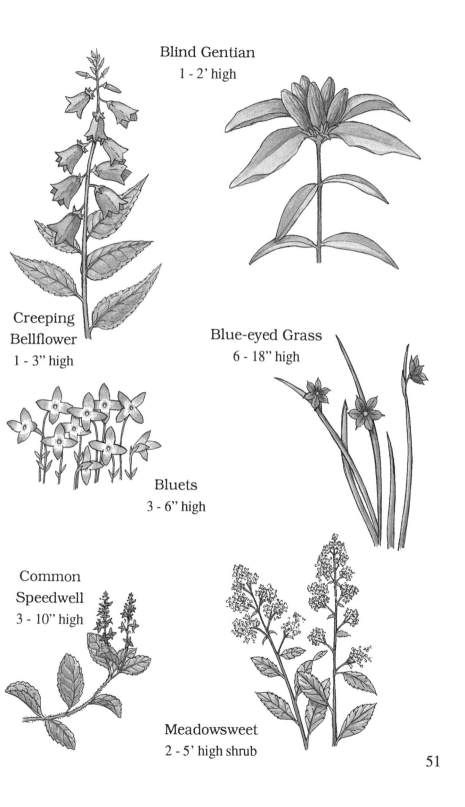

Blind Gentian
1 - 2' high

Creeping
Bellflower
1 - 3" high

Blue-eyed Grass
6 - 18" high

Bluets
3 - 6" high

Common
Speedwell
3 - 10" high

Meadowsweet
2 - 5' high shrub

51

Fireweed (July - September)

Showy clusters of large, **scarlet-red** flowers at the top of this tall plant. Leaves are long, thin, lance-shaped, green on top and pale beneath. Found on roadsides, in fields, clearings and burned-over areas.

Steeplebush (July - September)

Fuzzy cluster of **rose-pink** flowers in a "steeple" at top of shrubby plant. Leaves are oblong with toothed edges and white, woolly underneath. Stems also woolly. Found in fields and pastures.

Sheep Laurel (Lambkill) (June - July)

Pink, saucer-shaped flowers cluster around stem (not at the top). Leaves are dull green and lighter beneath, drooping below flowers. Leaves on top are lighter green and erect. Shrub. Found in pastures, woods and bogs. Poisonous to livestock.

Columbine (April - July)

Nodding, **scarlet-red**, irregular flowers with yellow centers and long, protruding stamens. Each petal has long spur in the back. Leaves on stem have 3 lobed leaflets. Long-stemmed, compound leaves accompany flower stems. Found in rocky woods, on ledges and open slopes.

Common Milkweed (June - August)

Small, **pink**, sweet-smelling flowers in thick clusters on top of the plant. Flowers grow to bumpy, green pods that burst with downy seeds in the fall. Large leaves are broad, pointed and woolly underneath, like stems. Broken stems leak sticky, white juice. Found in fields, roadsides.

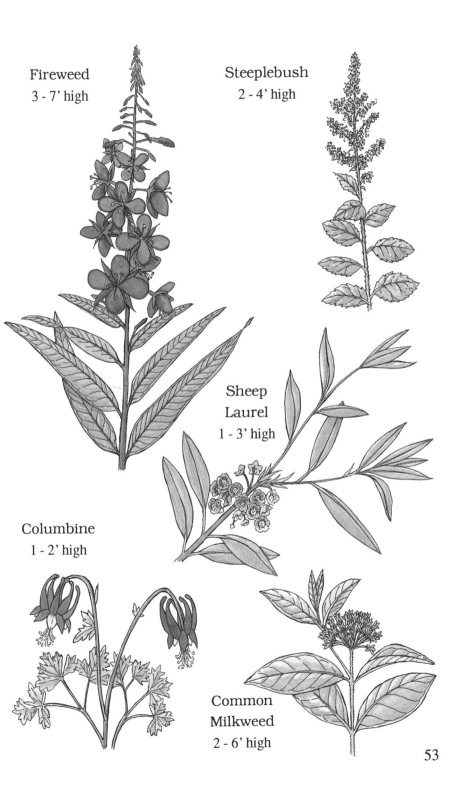

Fireweed
3 - 7' high

Steeplebush
2 - 4' high

Sheep
Laurel
1 - 3' high

Columbine
1 - 2' high

Common
Milkweed
2 - 6' high

53

Common Evening Primrose (June - September)

Large, **yellow**, lemon-scented flowers clustered on top of plant. Four petals. Leaves are long, lance-shaped, tooth-edged and alternate on hairy, purple-tinted stem. Found in fields, roadsides. Blooms in the evening until noon the next day. Resembles day-blooming sundrops.

St. Johnswort (June - September)

Clusters of small, **yellow** flowers on branched top of plant. Flower petals have small black dots along edge. Leaves are 1 - 2" long, oblong and arranged opposite on stem. Found in fields and on roadsides.

Common Mullein (June - September)

Spike-like cluster of **yellow** flowers tightly packed on erect, woolly stem. Five-petaled flowers only open a few at a time. Large, gray-green leaves are woolly and basally arranged. Smaller leaves arranged in a whorl up stem. Found in fields, roadsides.

Coltsfoot (April - June)

Yellow, dandelion-like flower about one inch across on scaly stem. Appears in early spring followed by large (3 - 7" wide), heart-shaped, toothed leaves. Found in damp soil, by streams and river banks.

Trout Lily (April - June)

Nodding, lily-like flower with 3 petals, 3 sepals all curved backward. Flower is **yellow inside and bronze outside** on single leafless stalk. Leaves are long, elliptical and pointed at the end with brown mottling. Found growing in groups in moist woods and meadows.

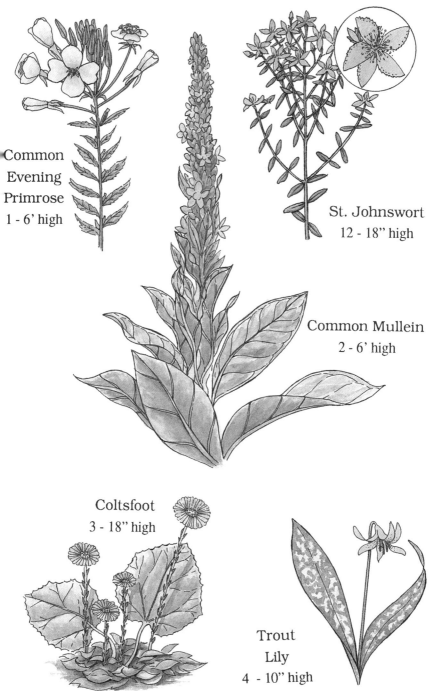

Common
Evening
Primrose
1 - 6' high

St. Johnswort
12 - 18" high

Common Mullein
2 - 6' high

Coltsfoot
3 - 18" high

Trout
Lily
4 - 10" high

55

Queen Anne's Lace (Wild Carrot) (June - September)
Flowers are tiny and **white** in a flat-topped lacy cluster called an umbel, with one dark reddish-brown floret in the center. Stem is hairy. Leaves are long, fern-like and smell like carrots. Found in dry fields, roadsides.

White Baneberry (May - June)
Tiny, **white** flowers tightly clustered in a spike on thick, individual flower stalks. Large leaves spread into many oval, pointed-end leaflets with toothed edges. Forms white berry clusters, each with distinct purple eye. Found in woods and thickets. **Red Baneberry** is similar but bears red berries.

Tall Meadow Rue (June - August)
Tiny flowers are made up of stiff, **light green to white** plumes of stamen (no petals) arranged in puffy clusters on a long stem. Leaves are broken up into oval, toothed leaflets (1" long). Found in moist meadows, swamps and sometimes on rocky wooded slopes.

Hobblebush (April -June)
White flowers with five petals arranged in a cluster with larger (about 1") flowers on the outside and smaller flowers grouped inside. Leaves are large (3 - 6") and heart-shaped, arranged opposite on woody stem. Found in moist woods.

Canada Mayflower (May - June)
Tiny, **white** star-shaped flowers form a dense cluster at top of plant. Two or three long, ribbed leaves, heart-shaped at base, cling to stem below blossoms. Stem often seems to zig-zag where leaves attach. Found in woodlands and clearings. Can carpet forest floor.

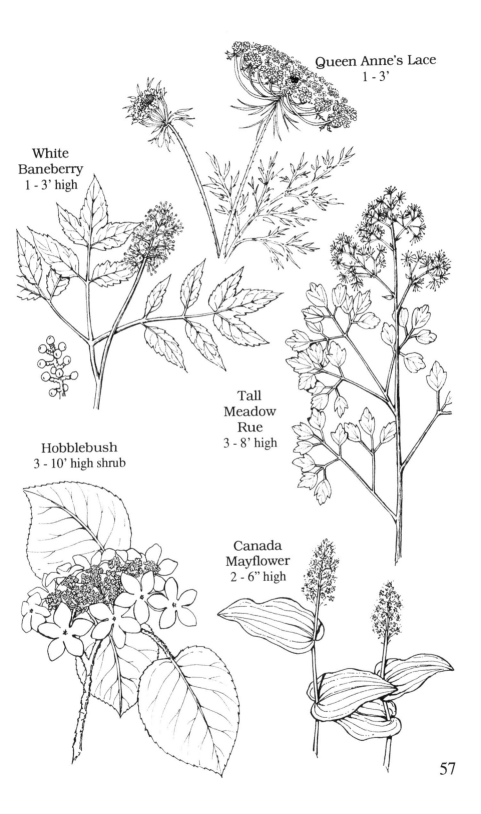

Queen Anne's Lace
1 - 3'

White
Baneberry
1 - 3' high

Tall
Meadow
Rue
3 - 8' high

Hobblebush
3 - 10' high shrub

Canada
Mayflower
2 - 6" high

57

Foamflower (May - June)

Many tiny **white** flowers with distinct stamens cluster along a leafless stem in a "foamy" spray. The leaves are basally arranged, heart-shaped, with toothed edges, shallow lobes. Found in rich woods in large groups.

Bladder Campion (May - August)

White flowers have distinct swollen area (calyx) behind petals that have **pink veins**. Flowers arranged in loose clusters on top of plant. Leaves are oblong to lance-shaped, arranged opposite on stem. Found in fields and along roadsides.

Marsh Marigold (Cowslip) (April - June)

Flowers have 5-10 glossy, **yellow** petal-like sepals (no true petals) with central spray of stamens and pistils on long erect stems. Heart-shaped leaves with scalloped edges arranged basally and on stem. Found in wet areas.

Yarrow (June - September)

Tiny, **white** flowers grouped into a flat-topped cluster at the top of woolly stem. Grayish-green leaves are feathery and fern-like alternately arranged on stem. Aromatic leaves. Found in fields and along roadsides.

Sarsaparilla (May - June)

Sprays of tiny, **green** flowers on leafless stalk. Ovate, toothed leaves on three-branched stem stand above flowers. Found in open woodlands.

Pearly Everlasting (July - September)

Flowers are small, **white**, round heads with small yellow tuft in center, clustered at top of woolly stem. Leaves are long and narrow, alternately arranged and woolly underneath. Found in dry fields, roadsides, yards.

Common Fleabane (May - August)

Small (1"), **white to lavender** flowers with yellow center in loose clusters on branched, hairy stems. Leaves basal and alternate up stem, toothed, oblong to lance-shaped, clasping stem at base of leaf. Found in fields and open woods.

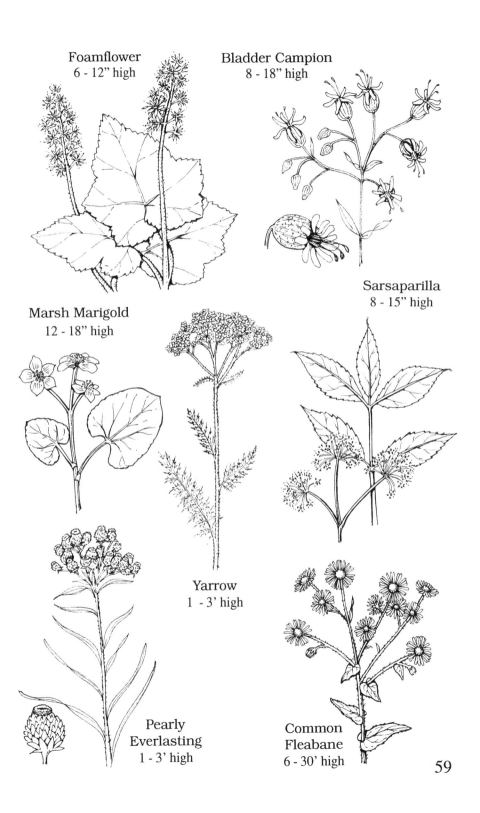

Foamflower
6 - 12" high

Bladder Campion
8 - 18" high

Sarsaparilla
8 - 15" high

Marsh Marigold
12 - 18" high

Yarrow
1 - 3' high

Pearly
Everlasting
1 - 3' high

Common
Fleabane
6 - 30' high

59

Mammals

There are about 55 different species of mammals in Vermont.
Mammals can be the most difficult animals to spot in the wild.
Most are nocturnal or only active at twilight or in early morning.
They are wary of humans, avoiding populated areas. Mammals
that are active during the day include squirrels and chipmunks,
with occasional sightings of moose, white-tailed deer, coyote, fox
and raccoon.

Never approach wild mammals. Observe them from a distance
only. Rabies has been found among certain species in Vermont,
particularly in red fox, skunk and raccoon. If these animals are
active in daylight and exhibit unusual behavior, they may be rabid
and can be aggressive. Bats can also carry rabies, but healthy
populations are beneficial because they consume large quantities
of insects. Screening attic vents can help keep bats from roosting
in homes.

Some identifying features of mammals are their tail, ear and
body shapes, colors and size. Length measurements include tail.

Moose

Animal Tracks

7"

White-tailed Deer

3"

Coyote

2 - 3"

Fox

1³/₄"

Raccoon

4"

White-footed Mouse

⁷/₈"

Gray Squirrel

2¹/₂"

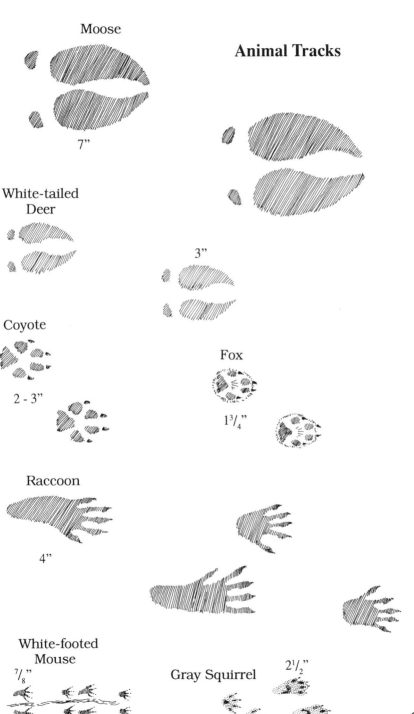

Moose

Gray to dark-brown with long legs, humped shoulders higher than tail end. Large snout droops down. Males can reach 1400 lbs. and have huge palmate antlers that are shed in winter. Feeds on stems, twigs, water plants. Found in wet forests, swamplands. Increasing in numbers in Vermont.

White-tailed Deer

Brown in summer, gray in winter. Males reach 200 lbs. and have spiked antlers shed in winter. Travel in small groups. Active mostly at twilight though can be seen all times of day, feeding on twigs, grass, acorns. Found in forests, farms and open brushy areas.

Black Bear

Vary in color but most are black in Vermont. Tan to brown muzzle. Males reach 300 lbs, females 150 lbs. Active mostly at night, feeding on small mammals, fruits, nuts, insects, carrion. Found in old-growth forests, burned-over areas and swamp lands.

Bobcat

Gray to reddish-brown with black spots on top, lighter underneath. Dark bars on front legs, face and top of short tail. Ears slightly tufted, cheeks ruffed. Solitary. Up to 45 lbs. Active nights, feeding on birds and small mammals: mice, squirrels, woodchucks and hares. Occasionally prey on deer. Found in forests, swamps. Rare in Vermont.

Lynx

Stockier than bobcat. Tawny with black hairs, short tail with black tip. Long, black ear tufts, cheek ruffs and large, furry feet. Active nights, feeding on snowshoe hares. Found in thick forests and swamps. Very rare.

Moose
6 - 9' long

White-tailed
Deer
4 - 6' long

Black Bear
5 - 6' long

Bobcat
$2^1/_2$ - 4' long

Lynx
$2^1/_2$ - $3^1/_2$'

63

Raccoon

Silvery-brown with dark-ringed, bushy tail, black mask. Up to 30 lbs. Active at night. Feeds on fruits, plants and small animals. Found in deciduous forests, marshes and residential areas.

Coyote

Frost gray to brown and paler underneath, bushy, drooping tail with black tip. Up to 55 lbs. More active at night. Scavenger, but may take small mammals and even deer. Found in open woodlands and fields.

Red Fox

Reddish above, white below, bushy tail with white tip. Narrow pointed muzzle. Up to 17 lbs. Active nights, mornings. Feeds on bugs, fruits, small animals. Found in open woods, fields.

Gray Fox

Frosted, gray above, white throat and belly, reddish on chest, under tail, and back of head. Black on each side of muzzle. Long, bushy tail, black tip. Up to 14 lbs. Active nights, twilight. Feeds on small animals, fruits, nuts. Found in deciduous forests, brushy places.

Fisher

Long, slender body, brown fur, frosted hairs on head, neck, shoulders. Long, bushy tail. Up to 16 lbs. Solitary. Active at twilight. Feeds on small mammals, birds, seeds, fruits. Can prey on porcupines. Found in forests. Rare. Resembles marten but larger.

Marten

Long, thin, brown, light throat patch. Up to 4 lbs. Active at twilight, lives in trees. Feeds on birds, squirrels, insects, nuts, fruits. Found in forests.

Raccoon
2 - 3' long

Coyote
$3^1/_2$ - $4^1/_2$'

Red Fox
2 - $3^1/_2$'

Gray Fox
$2^1/_2$ - $3^3/_4$'

Marten
$1^1/_2$ - $2^1/_4$'

Fisher
$2^1/_2$ - $3^1/_2$'

65

Mink

Long, thin, dark brown body with white chin and bushy tail. Up to 3 lbs. Solitary. Active at night, feeding on birds, fish, frogs and small mammals. Found in wetland areas, along streams and lakes.

Long-tailed Weasel

Long, slender body, brown above, lighter below in summer, turning white in winter. Long, thin tail *about half body length* with black tip all year. Weighs 4 - 9 oz. Solitary. Active day and night, hunting. Found in open forests, fields and farms. Longer tail than ermine.

Ermine (short-tailed weasel)

Long, slender body, brown above, lighter below, turning white in winter. Long, thin tail *less than half body length* with black tip all year. Up to 4 oz. only. Solitary. Active day and night, hunting any small animal. Hides kills for later feeding. Found in thick forests, fields, farms.

Striped Skunk

Stout, black body with 2 white stripes down back and bushy tail. Up to 12 lbs. Solitary. Active nights, feeding on mice, eggs, fruits, insects. Found in forests, fields and farmlands. When threatened, lifts tail and sprays strong, musky fluid that irritates the eyes.

River Otter

Long, sleek, dark brown body, silver-gray throat. Long, thick tail that tapers at the end, webbed feet. Up to 30 lbs. Active days, feeding mostly on fish and crayfish, also taking reptiles, amphibians. Occasionally preys on muskrat, beaver and birds. Often fishes under ice. Found in and along streams, lakes, ponds. Largest member of the weasel family left in Vermont.

Mink
$1/_2$ - $2^1/_2$'

Long-tailed
Weasel
11 - 21"

Winter coat for
long-tailed weasel
and ermine

Ermine
7 - 14"

Striped
Skunk
20 - 32"

River
Otter
3 - $4^1/_2$'

67

Short-tailed Shrew

Gray with very short tail, tiny eyes and pointed face (though blunter face than long-tailed species). Tail and feet have little hair. Up to .8 oz. Active day and night. Fierce hunter, feeding on insects, worms, mice, other shrews. Prey is often much larger than shrew. Saliva has poison that paralyzes prey. Found in woods, fields, wetlands.

Masked Shrew

Brown, slender body with long tail that is darker above and pale below with a dark tip. Small eyes, rounded forehead and pointed nose. Up to .25 oz. only. Active year round, mostly at night. Feeds on insects, spiders, earthworms and centipedes. Found in mixed forests, bogs and swamps.

Hairy-tailed Mole

Short, blackish-brown fur with purple sheen, tiny eyes hidden by fur, pointy nose. Hairy tail. Broad, sharp-clawed front feet that seem to come from shoulders. Up to 2.5 oz. More active during daylight, year round. Feeds on insects and worms in the soil. Found in and around underground tunnels in dry to moist soils.

Star-nosed Mole

Blackish-brown fur, small eyes, and distinct, fleshy "star" of short tentacles around nose. Scaly, ringed tail as long as body and with coarse hairs. Large paddle-like front feet with claws. Up to 2 oz. Active day and night, year round. Feeds on insects, worms and small water animals such as crayfish, frogs and fish. Found in wet forests or meadows near water, swamps, marshes. Swims well.

Short-tailed
Shrew
$3^1/_2$ - 5"

Masked
Shrew
3 - 4"

Hairy-tailed
Mole
$4^1/_2$ - 6"

Star-nosed
Mole
7 - 8"

Eastern Cottontail

Brownish-gray body, white feet, tail brown above, white below, 3 in. ears. Up to 3 lbs. Active nights, early mornings and evenings. Feeds on green plants, twigs, buds and bark. Found in fields, thickets and wooded areas.

Snowshoe Hare

Golden-brown on top, lighter below in summer, white in winter with black-rimmed, 3 - 4 inch ears. Large, furry feet allowing travel in deep snows. Active nights. Feeds on twigs, buds, grass, bark. Found in forests, thickets and swamps.

Beaver

Dark brown, large, flat, scaly tail, webbed hind feet, small eyes, ears. Largest rodent in U.S. Up to 110 lbs. Active nights,  eating twigs, bark, cutting trees. Found in and along rivers, marshes, lakes, ponds. Builds lodges and dams.

Muskrat

Glossy, brown above, silvery below, long, hairless tail, webbed back feet. Up to 4 lbs. Spends much of its time in the water, eating fish, frogs, water plants. Found in marshes, lakes, streams and ponds.

Woodchuck

Frosted brown to black on top, lighter beneath, bushy tail, small ears. 6 - 12 lbs. Active days feeding on grass, clover, berries, garden plants. Found in fields, forests, brushy areas and along roadways. Largest member of the squirrel family.

Eastern
Cottontail
1 - 1$\frac{1}{2}$' long

winter coat

Snowshoe Hare
1$\frac{3}{4}$' long

Beaver
3 - 4'

Muskrat
1$\frac{1}{2}$ -2'

Woodchuck
1$\frac{1}{2}$ - 2$\frac{1}{2}$'

71

Eastern Chipmunk

Red-brown on top, white below. White stripe under eyes and down sides, bordered by black stripes. Runs with tail up. Up to 3 oz. Active days feeding on seeds, fruits, nuts, insects. Found in forests and brushy areas. Goes into burrow in winter but not true hibernator.

Northern Flying Squirrel

Small squirrel, large eyes. Brown above, white below with loose fold of skin between front and back legs that spreads to enable it to glide from tree to tree. Active nights feeding on nuts, fruits, mushrooms and seeds. Nests in tree holes. Found in forests.

Eastern Gray Squirrel

Gray above, lighter below, flat, bushy tail with white-tipped hairs around edge. 1-2 lbs. Active dawn and dusk feeding on fruits, seeds, nuts and bark. Found in forests with nut trees, residential areas. Lives and nests in trees. Very agile climber but also active on the ground.

Red Squirrel

Reddish-gray on top, lighter below with black line along each side. Half the size of gray squirrel. Up to $8^{1}/_{2}$ oz. Active days living mostly in trees. Feeds on conifer seeds cutting green cones into piles for storage. Also eats buds, mushrooms, nuts and bark. Found in coniferous and mixed forests.

Porcupine

Stout body covered with long, grizzled hairs intermixed with long, barbed quills. Short legs and lumbering walk. Up to 20 lbs. Active at night, feeding on twigs, buds and bark. Found on the ground and up in trees. Attracted to salt on the roads. Found in mixed forests.

Eastern Chipmunk
8 - 11' long

Northern Flying Squirrel
10 - 15' long

Eastern Gray Squirrel
$1\frac{1}{2}$ - $1\frac{3}{4}$' long

Red Squirrel
12" long

Porcupine
2 - 3' long

73

Deer Mouse

Grayish-brown on top, white below. Tail is dark above and white below (bicolored) with white tuft at tip and longer than body length. Nests in trees, homes and in ground. Up to 1 oz. Active at night, feeding on nuts, seeds, fruits, insects, worms and fungi. Found in fields and forests.

White-footed Mouse

Reddish-brown on top with darker stripe down the middle, white below. Tail is bicolored like deer mouse but pale, not white below and shorter than body length. Up to 1 oz. Active nights. Feeds on seeds, nuts, fruit, insects. Found in forests and brushy lowland areas.

Meadow Vole

Brown on top, lighter below, even on tail. Rounded body, small ears, short tail, barely a third of body length. Up to $1\frac{1}{2}$ oz. Active at twilight. Travels in tunnels in the grass. Feeds on grass, seeds, bark and insects. Found in fields, swamps, marshes and moist woodlands.

Woodland Vole

Short orange-brown fur, small eyes and ears. Tail is very short (1"). Up to $1\frac{1}{4}$ oz. Active day and night feeding on plants, seeds, fruits and bark. Found in forest leaf litter.

Little Brown Bat

Glossy golden-brown fur. Long hairs on hind feet. Up to 1 oz. Active nights feeding on flying insects. Found roosting in buildings and trees.

Hoary Bat

Yellowish-brown fur. Small, rounded ears. Larger of the Vermont bats. Up to $1\frac{1}{2}$ oz. Active at night, feeding on flying insects. Found in the summer season in wooded areas.

74

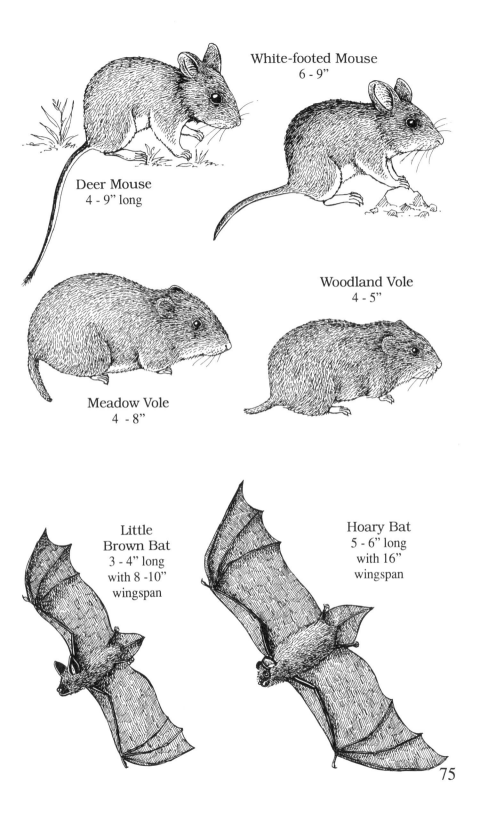

White-footed Mouse
6 - 9"

Deer Mouse
4 - 9" long

Woodland Vole
4 - 5"

Meadow Vole
4 - 8"

Little
Brown Bat
3 - 4" long
with 8 -10"
wingspan

Hoary Bat
5 - 6" long
with 16"
wingspan

Insects

Insects are found everywhere in the world and they are keenly adapted for their short season in Vermont. Many kinds of insects in Vermont will seek out humans and other animals to feast upon their rich supply of blood.

Insects have no bones, instead they have a soft body surrounded by a hard shell called an "exoskeleton." Their bodies are divided into three segments: head, thorax and abdomen. They have two antennae and six legs attached to their thorax. Most have two pairs of wings on their thorax, but some have one pair or none. Many insects you'll see will be immature; these are called larvae. Larvae do not have the classic insect characteristics described above.

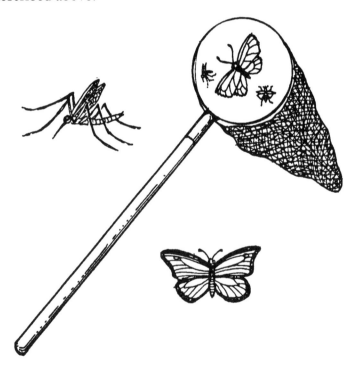

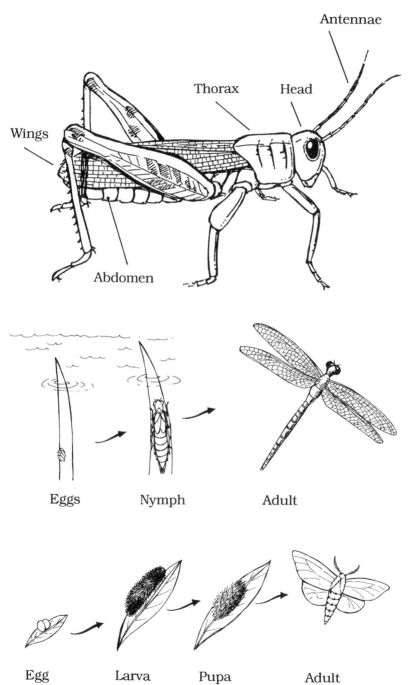

Antennae

Thorax   Head

Wings

Abdomen

Eggs   Nymph   Adult

Egg   Larva   Pupa   Adult

77

Found in meadows and open areas:

Bumble Bee

Black and yellow, hairy, orange pollen collectors on legs. Pollinators of clover and other plants. Found in fields, pastures, orchards and yards, nests underground. Stings.

Yellow Jacket

Black and yellow. Build nests on buildings, rock walls or underground. Can sting fiercely when bothered. Found in orchards, fields and on the edge of forests.

Firefly

Brown wings rimmed in yellow, red plate behind head with black spot in center. Tail end lights on summer nights to attract mate. Feeds on insects, worms, snails. Found in fields, yards.

Grasshopper

Many kinds with varying sizes. Green, yellow-brown body and wings with large back legs for jumping. Garden and farm pest, eating plants. Found in fields, yards, farms and roadsides. Common.

Katydid

Green with long back legs, large leaf-like wings and long antennae. Feeds on plants, trees. *Katydid* call on summer nights. Found in fields, yards and roadsides.

Field Cricket

Brown, large head, short wings and two long "tails." Eats plants, insects. Active at night making shrill song. Found in fields, yards and can invade houses in late summer.

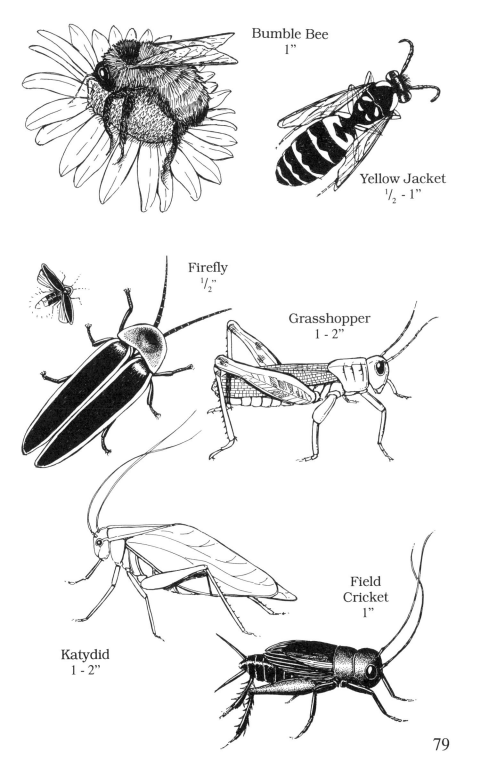

Bumble Bee
1"

Yellow Jacket
$1/2$ - 1"

Firefly
$1/2$"

Grasshopper
1 - 2"

Katydid
1 - 2"

Field
Cricket
1"

79

Ladybird Beetle

Red beetle, black spots. Eats insects, mainly aphids. Found in fields, yards, gardens and roadsides. Hibernates under rocks and logs (or enters homes) in winter. Common.

Daddy Long Legs

Small body with eight long, thin legs. Spider, not characterized as an insect. Eats insects. Found around homes in yards, gardens, forests and fields.

Ground Beetle

Shiny, black, long body. Rounded wing covers with lengthwise grooves. Eats other insects. Found in woods, gardens, under stones and boards.

Tent Caterpillar

Caterpillars swarm in thick webs in tree branches in the spring. Adult moths are brown with white stripes on front wings. Harmful to fruit trees. Can damage whole forests.

Walking Stick

Thin, brownish-green with twig-like body and long, thin legs. No wings, long antennae. Blends well on trees making it hard to detect. Active at night, feeding on tree leaves. Can cause damage. Found in deciduous forests and yards.

Praying Mantis

Green to tan, long, slender body, longer wings. Feeds on other insects, including other mantises. Solitary. Has powerful vision and the ability to turn its head to search for prey. Found in meadows and fields.

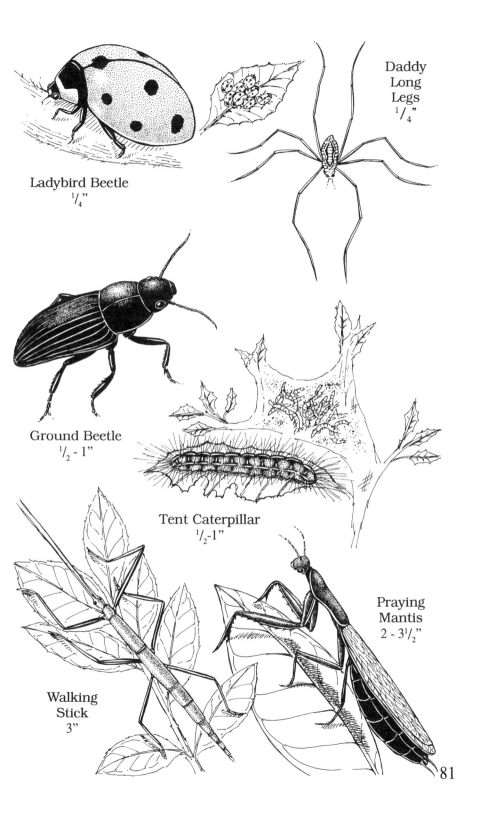

Ladybird Beetle
$^1/_4$"

Daddy
Long
Legs
$^1/_4$"

Ground Beetle
$^1/_2$ - 1"

Tent Caterpillar
$^1/_2$-1"

Praying
Mantis
2 - 3$^1/_2$"

Walking
Stick
3"

81

Found in and near water:

Water Strider
Black with a thin, flat, body and long thin legs. Usually wingless. Skates on water surface. Feeds on insects. Found on ponds and streams.

Whirligig Beetle
Black, shiny ovals. Gather in swarms on water surface, swimming in circles. Feeds on insects, snails, mites. Found on ponds and streams, especially along edges. Swims in circles when threatened.

Water Boatman
Gray-brown, long, oval body with cross-hatched pattern on wing covers. Back legs are flattened and paddle-like, fringed with hair. Feeds on algae. Found in ponds and attracted to algae in bird baths, fountains. Zig-zag swimming pattern.

Giant Water Bug
Large, brown, elongated oval body. Flattened shape. Large front legs catch prey. Hind legs flattened for swimming. Feed on small fish, frogs, tadpoles and insects. Found in ponds. May play dead, but bite painfully.

Backswimmer
Varies in color from tan or reddish to green on top. Swims on its back showing legs above the water. Front legs grasp prey, back legs flat with hair fringe for paddling. Feeds on insects. Found in ponds and slow-moving streams. Bite feels like a bee sting.

Eastern Dobsonfly
Long, tannish-brown body covered with long, clear, veined wings. Males have long, hooked mandibles. Found on vegetation near fast-moving water. Larvae live underwater for 3 years and are prized bait.

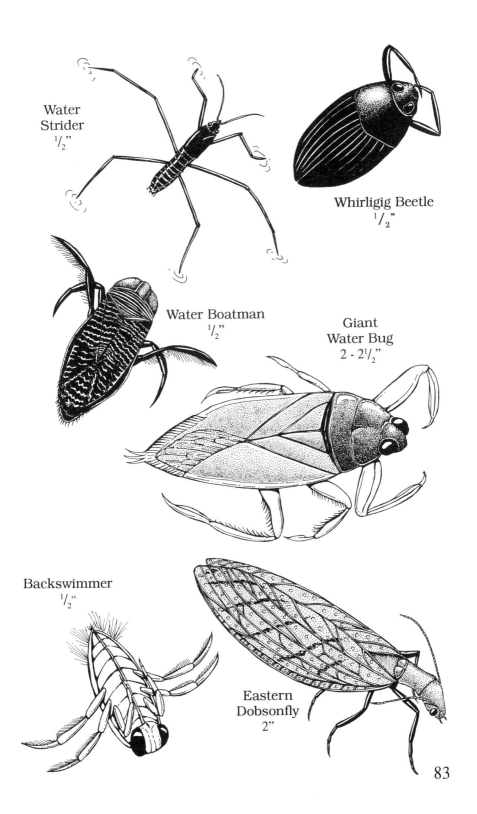

Water
Strider
$1/_2$"

Whirligig Beetle
$1/_2$"

Water Boatman
$1/_2$"

Giant
Water Bug
2 - $2 1/_2$"

Backswimmer
$1/_2$"

Eastern
Dobsonfly
2"

83

Mayfly

Large variation in size. Reddish-brown with large, clear wings distinctly veined. Two long, trailing tails. Only feeds as a nymph in water (adults have no mouth parts for feeding). Adults dance above water, mate, lay eggs and die in a few short hours.

Dragonflies:

Many sizes and colors. All have large wings with powerful, buzzing flight. Rests with wings spread. Feeds on insects. Found near wet areas, along streams, ponds and marshes.

Green Darner

Green thorax with bluish-gray abdomen. Found near ponds and slow-moving streams.

Brown Darner

Brown body with 2 large yellow spots on thorax and front margin of wings. Found in shadows on the edge of streams.

Twelve Spot Skimmer

Brown head and thorax with white glaze on abdomen. Three brown spots on each wing. Males have white spots between brown spots.

Swift Long-winged Skimmer

Blue body. Wings clear or hazy with brown glaze toward ends. Found over large ponds and wide streams.

Elisa Skimmer

Black body with red patches on abdomen. Wings with black spots at tips and in middle with dark, reddish-black area at the base of each wing. Found in marshes, ponds and slow-moving streams.

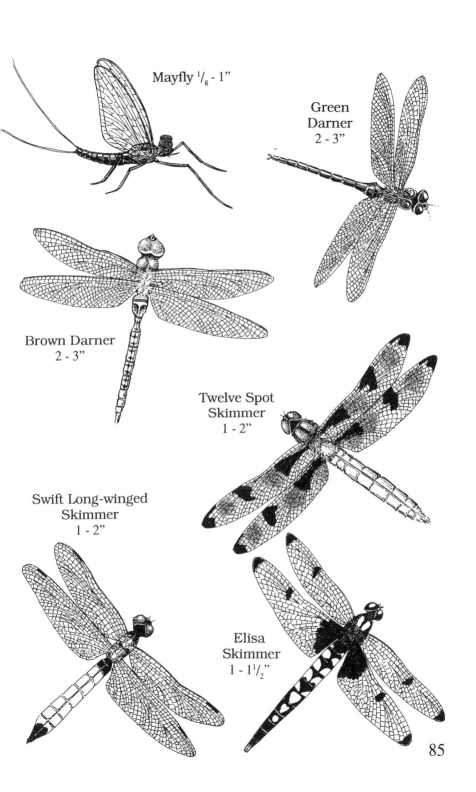

Mayfly ⅛ - 1"

Green
Darner
2 - 3"

Brown Darner
2 - 3"

Twelve Spot
Skimmer
1 - 2"

Swift Long-winged
Skimmer
1 - 2"

Elisa
Skimmer
1 - 1½"

85

Damselfly

Blue with black dashes down back. Rests briefly on water plants with wings folded back. Feeds on insects. Found near wet areas, along streams, ponds. Smaller than dragonflies.

Butterflies and Moths:

Luna Moth

White body, green wings with purple front margins, hind wings have long green tails, brown markings. Caterpillar feeds on tree leaves. Found in deciduous forest.

Tiger Swallowtail

Yellow and black striped wings with "tails," black edge with one red patch on each side of hind wings and blue patches in between. Caterpillar feeds on wild cherry leaves. Found in forests, fields.

Spicebush Swallowtail

Dark front wings have yellow spots on outer margin. Outer side of dark hind wings have one red spot on each side and blue spots in between. Inner side of hind wing has orange spots. Caterpillar feeds on leaves. Found in woods, fields, and gardens.

Black Swallowtail

Dark wings with rows of yellow spots. On the inside edge of each hind wing there is an orange eye spot with black center and a row of blue patches between the rows of yellow spots. Caterpillar may be a garden pest. Found in fields, farms and gardens.

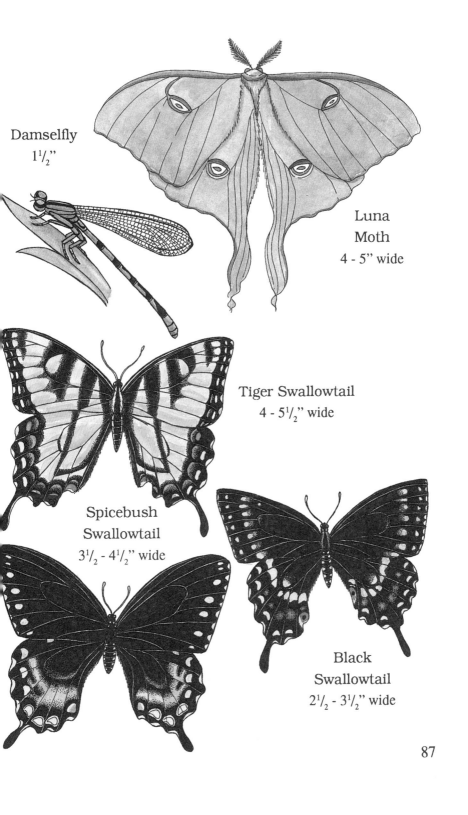

Damselfly
1$\frac{1}{2}$"

Luna
Moth
4 - 5" wide

Tiger Swallowtail
4 - 5$\frac{1}{2}$" wide

Spicebush
Swallowtail
3$\frac{1}{2}$ - 4$\frac{1}{2}$" wide

Black
Swallowtail
2$\frac{1}{2}$ - 3$\frac{1}{2}$" wide

Monarch Butterfly

Orange wings with black veins and edges peppered
with white spots. Caterpillar is black, yellow,
white striped and feeds on milkweeds. Found in
open fields. Poisonous to birds. Only butterfly
that migrates yearly north to south.

Viceroy

Darker orange with thicker black veins and margins
than monarch. White spots in margin and on front
wings surrounded by black. Caterpillar feeds on willow
and poplar. Found in marshes, meadows, riversides and
lake shores.

Mourning Cloak

Brown, iridescent wings with yellow, irregular edges
and inside row of blue spots. Drab underside acts as
camouflage against tree bark. Caterpillar feeds on willow and poplar leaves.
Found along forest borders, rivers and fields.

Red Admiral

Dark wings with orange band across each front wing and along edge of hind
wings. White spots on front wing above orange band. Mottled below. Caterpillar feeds on nettles. Found along forest edges, shorelines, rivers, roads, parks
and fields.

White Admiral

Dark wings with wide, white band across each wing, rows of orange spots,
rows of bluish dashes and orange spots closer to body on all four wings.
Caterpillar feeds on birch, willow and poplar. Found in upland hardwood
forests.

Monarch Butterfly
3 - 4" wide

Viceroy
$2\frac{1}{2}$ - 3" wide

Mourning Cloak
$2\frac{1}{2}$ - $3\frac{1}{2}$" wide

Red Admiral
$1\frac{3}{4}$ - $2\frac{1}{4}$" wide

White Admiral
3 - $3\frac{1}{2}$" wide

89

Painted Lady

Orange with black blotches. Dark edges on front wings with white dashes along edge. White bar and spots on darker front portion of front wing. Hind wing has black spots on top side of wings and blue spots on bottom side. Caterpillar feeds on thistles. Found in meadows, fields and parks.

Meadow Fritillary

Orange with dark dots and dashes. No dark border on wing edges. Caterpillars feed on violets. Found in bogs, moist meadows and along streams.

Pearly Crescentspot

Orange with black spots and splotches and wide black wing edges. Underside is cream-colored with fine brown lines. Caterpillar feeds on asters. Found in moist meadows, roadsides and along streams. Common.

Silvery Checkerspot

Brown with orange squares on all four wings and white dashes along wing edges. Caterpillar feeds on sunflowers. Found along roads, lakes and meadows. Resembles many small butterflies, hard to make positive identification.

Common Sulfur

Light yellow with wide black wing edges. Female has yellow spots in black border. Underneath is greenish-yellow. Caterpillar feeds on clover. Found in pastures, fields and meadows.

Eastern Tailed Blue

Bright silvery-blue with dark edges. Hind wings have orange spot with black border at bottom and tiny tail. Caterpillar feeds on clover and wild peas. Found in fields and open sites like railroad tracks.

Painted Lady
2 - 4$\frac{1}{4}$" wide

Meadow Fritillary
1$\frac{1}{2}$" - 1$\frac{3}{4}$" wide

Pearly Crescentspot
1 - 1$\frac{1}{2}$" wide

Silvery
Checkerspot
1$\frac{1}{2}$" wide

Common Sulfur
1$\frac{1}{2}$-2" wide

Eastern
Tailed Blue
1" wide

Amphibians

Amphibians have soft, moist skin and no scales. Most lay soft eggs underwater. They are usually found in or near water and burrow into the mud or leaf litter when the weather turns cold to emerge again in the spring.

Red Eft (Eastern Newt)

Bright orange-red with spots. Active in wet weather, feeding on insects. Found in swamps, ditches and wet forest floors.

Dusky Salamander

Dark mottled skin with light patch behind eye down to jaw. Feeds on worms and insects. Found in springs, small streams and muddy areas.

Spotted Salamander

Black, stocky body with two rows of yellow spots from head to tip of tail. Feeds on insects and worms. Found in wetlands, ponds, ditches and moist woods. Feeds under leaf litter and soil so is rarely noticed.

Two-lined Salamander

Yellow-bronze to red with two stripes down back from eyes to tail. Area between stripes mottled with dark spots. Found in brooks, wetlands.

Bullfrog

Greenish-yellow body with darker mottling, big eardrums called "tympani" and webbed back feet. Active at night, feeding on crayfish, frogs, minnows and earthworms. Found in large ponds, lakes and rivers. Deep *Jug-o-rum* call.

Pickerel Frog

Smooth tan to greenish-brown skin with rows of darker squares running down back. Active at night, feeding on worms, insects and snails. Found in ponds and bogs with plant life. Steady, low croak.

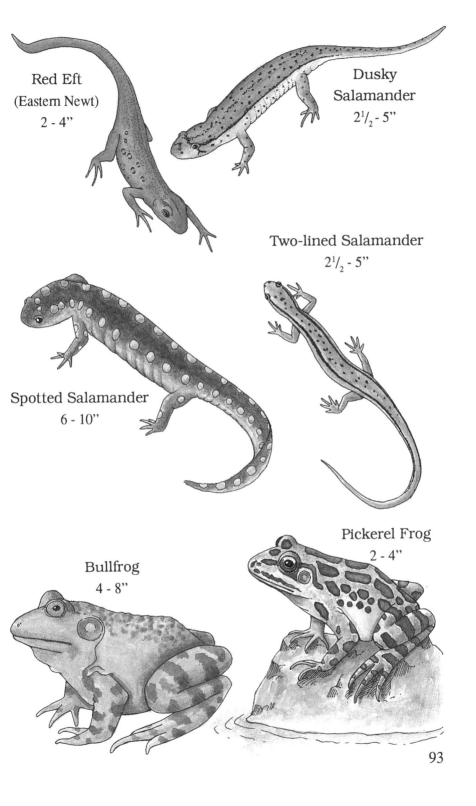

Red Eft
(Eastern Newt)
2 - 4"

Dusky
Salamander
$2^1/_2$ - 5"

Two-lined Salamander
$2^1/_2$ - 5"

Spotted Salamander
6 - 10"

Bullfrog
4 - 8"

Pickerel Frog
2 - 4"

93

Green Frog

Green with yellow throat on male. Large eardrum (tympani) and shoulder ridges. Active at night feeding on insects. Found in ponds, lakes and wetlands.

Spring Peeper

Tan, gray to brown with X-shaped mark on back. Active at night with high-pitched whistle and trill sound. Out early in the spring. Found in woodland ponds and swamps.

Wood Frog

Brown to pinkish skin with dark mask around eyes and light stripe on upper lip. Dark patch on chest inside each front leg. Active during the day feeding on insects. First frog out in the spring. Found in moist woodlands.

Gray Treefrog

Rough skin varies in color from brown to gray to green, always with dark blotches on back. Inside of thighs yellow to orange. Feeds on insects. Found in forests and thickets near water. Clings to branches.

American Toad

Gray to brown with large lumps and dark spots and light line down middle. Active mostly at night. Feeds on insects, worms and slugs. Protects itself by burrowing. Also can exude fluid through its skin that is poisonous if ingested. Found everywhere from farms and woods to gardens. Common.

bullfrog

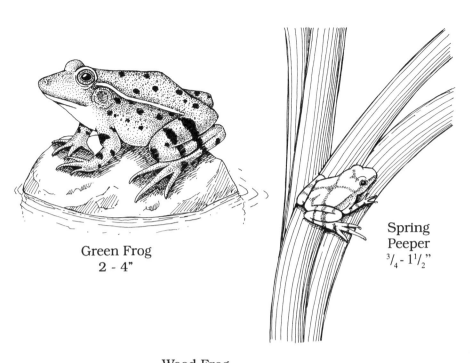

Green Frog
2 - 4"

Spring
Peeper
$^{3}/_{4}$ - $1^{1}/_{2}$"

Wood Frog
$1^{1}/_{2}$ - 3"

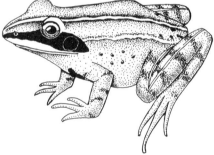

Gray Treefrog
$1^{1}/_{4}$ - $2^{1}/_{2}$"

American Toad
2 - $4^{1}/_{2}$"

95

Reptiles
have hard, dry skin, often covered with scales. Like amphibians they are usually found near water and burrow into the mud to overwinter. Because they are cold-blooded they are often seen sunning on rocks and logs. Using binoculars, this is a good way to observe reptiles.

Snakes in Vermont are mostly harmless though they can bite if handled. There is, however, a small population of eastern rattlesnakes (a poisonous species) in the rocky areas along Lake Champlain. Snake lengths vary and so a range of possible lengths is shown.

Garter Snake

Greenish-brown to black on top, yellow below. Light stripe runs along each side. Active during day, feeding on worms, frogs, small mammals and birds. Found in wet fields, marshes, woodlands, farms and yards.

Milk Snake

Grayish-tan with large brownish-red spots bordered in black along sides and back. Feeds on small rodents, birds and other snakes. Found in woodlands under rotten logs or leaf litter. Shy, seen mostly at night.

Eastern Ribbon Snake

Slender snake with three bright stripes running down brown body. Feeds on frogs, salamanders and fish. Found in wetlands and by ponds, often in bushes by water's edge. Glides across water's surface.

Brown Snake

Small, yellowish-brown with light band down center of body bordered by dark spots. Feeds on worms, slugs and snails. Found in woodlands and wetlands under logs, rocks and leaf litter. Out in daylight.

Garter Snake
18 - 48"

Milk Snake
12 - 60"

Eastern Ribbon Snake
18 - 44"

Brown
Snake
12 - 28"

97

Lizards are rare in Vermont with only one species represented.

Five-Lined Skink

Dark with five broad light stripes. Adults fade to brown. Tail is blue in juveniles fading to gray in adults. Found in woodland leaf litter. Eats insects, caterpillars, worms and spiders. Active during the day.

Turtles lay hard-shelled eggs in the soil. They have no teeth but use their sharp bill to cut up plants and small animals. They can bite.

Painted Turtle

Smooth, dark green to black shell with red edges. Yellow and red stripes on neck, legs and tail. Feeds on plants, insects and water animals. Found in slow-moving streams, rivers, lakes, ponds, marshes.

Snapping Turtle

Rough dark green to brown shell, usually covered with algae. Large powerful head and long spiked tail. Feeds on water animals. Found in fresh water pond, lakes and rivers. Burrows in mud bottoms. Can inflict serious bite when handled. Caution!

Eastern Box Turtle

Shell is dark green to brown with lighter mottling and high, boxy dome shape. Lives on land, hiding under logs or in mud, feeding on slugs, worms and fruit. Found in woodlands and pastures. Very rare.

Wood Turtle

Brown, rough shell with deep grooves. Neck and legs are reddish-orange. Feeds on worms, insects, fruits. Found in marshes, swamps, wet meadows, farm fields and woodlands. Has become rare from over-collection. Protected.

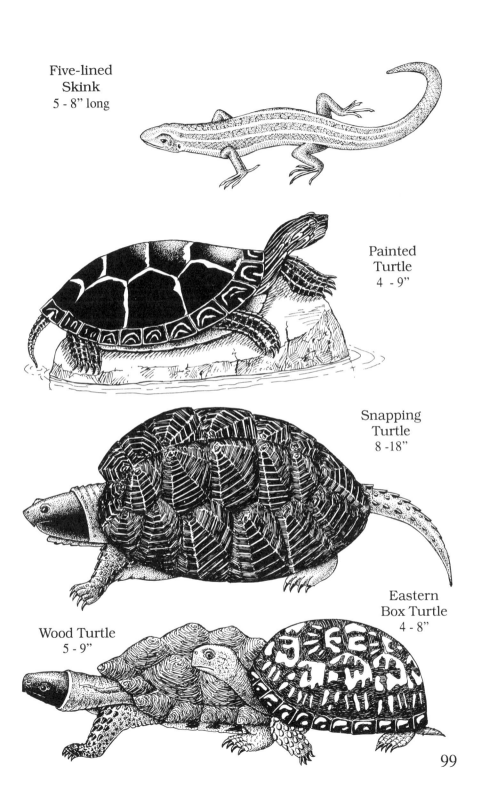

Five-lined
Skink
5 - 8" long

Painted
Turtle
4 - 9"

Snapping
Turtle
8 -18"

Eastern
Box Turtle
4 - 8"

Wood Turtle
5 - 9"

99

Trees

Trees are plants with a single, large, woody stem or trunk that grows to at least 15 feet at maturity. For the purpose of this book the trees are divided into two main groups:

Angiosperms are flowering plants that bear their seed inside a fruit. This huge group of plants includes the "deciduous" trees.

Deciduous trees lose their leaves every fall. Their flowers, leaves and fruits include many different shapes and sizes. Flowers can vary from blossoms to catkins, fruits from fleshy to woody. Leaves can have smooth or toothed edges and glossy or fuzzy surfaces. The most common types are shown below.

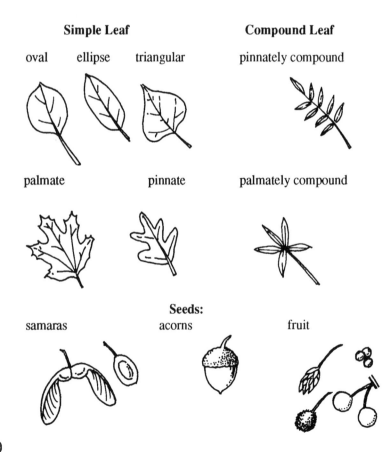

Simple Leaf			**Compound Leaf**
oval	ellipse	triangular	pinnately compound

palmate	pinnate	palmately compound

Seeds:

samaras	acorns	fruit

Gymnosperms, the second group, do not have flowers and bear seeds in a cone. These are the conifers that are represented in Vermont by the pine family (Pinaceae), which includes pines, tamaracks, spruces, firs and hemlocks, and the cedar family (Cupressaceae). These groups have needles for leaves. They all stay green year round except for the tamarack. These trees are identified by needle shape, number of needles in a cluster, and cone shape. See the examples below.

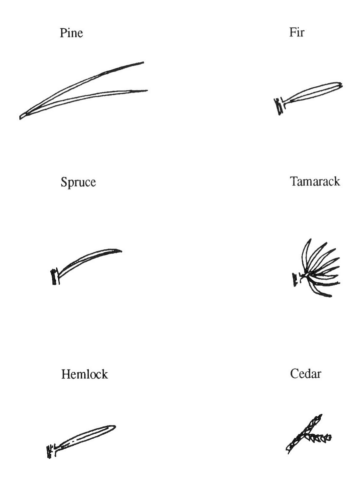

Pine

Fir

Spruce

Tamarack

Hemlock

Cedar

Deciduous Trees

Sugar Maple

Bark is gray and furrowed, growing scaly with age. Leaves are about 5 in. wide with 5 palmate lobes and toothed edge. Leaves turn yellow, red and orange in fall. Winged, U-shaped pairs of seeds called samaras. Sap collected in spring for maple syrup production.

Red Maple

Bark is gray and furrowed, growing scaley with age. Leaves are 5 in. wide, toothed and lobed with reddish stems. Leaf lobes are more pointed than sugar maples. Leaves turn red in the fall. Winged seeds.

Striped Maple

Bark smooth and green with white stripes. Leaves are large and rounded with three lobes and toothed edges. Leaves turn yellow in fall. Winged seeds.

Mountain Ash

Bark is light gray-brown and smooth growing scaly with age. Leaves are 6 - 8 in. long, pinnately compound with many rough-edged leaflets. Leaves are yellow-green. Small white flowers grow into clusters of orange berries. Birds feed on the berries.

Elm

Bark is gray with deep, forked ridges. Toothed leaves are 4 - 6 in. long, dark green, and rough above, soft hairs beneath and long, pointed, ellipse-shaped. Seeds are rounded samaras with flattened rim. Dutch elm disease has reduced the once abundant elm to a rare sight.

White Ash

Bark is gray with diamond-shaped ridges. Leaves are 8 - 12 in. long, pinnately compound with many oval leaflets. Leaves are dark green above and whitish below. Thin winged seeds hang in clusters.

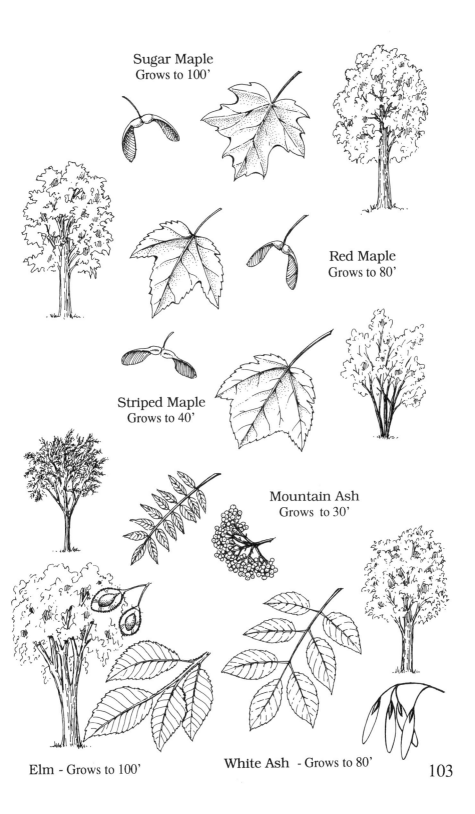

Sugar Maple
Grows to 100'

Red Maple
Grows to 80'

Striped Maple
Grows to 40'

Mountain Ash
Grows to 30'

Elm - Grows to 100'

White Ash - Grows to 80'

103

The **Willow family** (Salicaceae) is represented by several members in Vermont. These species are often mistaken for one another or commonly referred to simply as poplars (or "popples"). The following trees are usually included in that group with the least common actually being the balsam poplar.

Quaking Aspen

Bark whitish, smooth becoming gray and ridged with age. Leaves are 1 - 3 in. round and shiny green with fine teeth. Leaves grow on long, flattened stalks which produce a quaking motion in a breeze. Flowers are catkins and appear in early spring, before leaves.

Bigtooth Aspen

Bark is green in young trees, turning brown and ridged with age. Leaves are 2 - 4 in. large, dull green ovals with large rounded teeth. These teeth distinguish them from the smaller-toothed leaves of quaking aspen. Leaf stalks are flattened. Flowers are catkins that turn to cottony seeds.

Eastern Cottonwood

Huge, often branched trunk. Bark is green in young trees, turning gray and ridged with age. Leaves are 3 - 7 in., triangular, shiny green with rounded teeth. Flattened stalk. Flowers are catkins that turn to cottony seeds.

Balsam Poplar

Smooth, brown trunk growing furrowed with age. Leaves are 3 - 5 in. shiny green above, whitish below and rounded with pointed tip and rounded teeth. Flowers are catkins. Stems and buds have strong balsam odor.

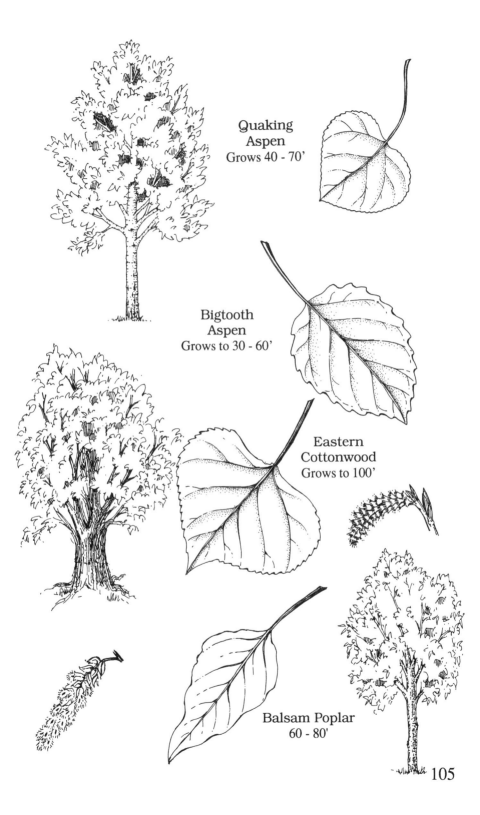

Quaking
Aspen
Grows 40 - 70'

Bigtooth
Aspen
Grows to 30 - 60'

Eastern
Cottonwood
Grows to 100'

Balsam Poplar
60 - 80'

105

Yellow Birch

Bark is shiny, yellow to bronze that ages into reddish brown. Leaves are 3 - 5 in., dull green, long, narrow ellipses with toothed edges. Leaves are hairy when young. Flowers are catkins that grow into small hairy cones.

Paper Birch

Bark is white and peeling with dark lines running around trunk. Leaves are 2 - 4 in. long, pointed, dull green ovals with teeth. Flowers are catkins that grow to small cones. Stripping bark damages trees; collect from fallen logs only.

Northern Red Oak

Bark is gray to black with scaly ridges. Leaves are darker green above, 5 - 8 in. long with 7 - 11 pointed lobes and teeth. Acorns are oval with small cup enclosing one-third of nut.

White Oak

Bark is light gray with ridges. Large leaves are greener above, 4 - 9 in. long with rounded lobes. Leaves are widest past the middle. Acorns have small cup and long nut.

Chokecherry

Bushy tree. Bark is shiny-brown with pale markings, becoming scaly with age. Leaves are wide ellipses with toothed edges coming to a point. 2 - 4 in. long and 1 - 2 in. wide. Small bitter cherries grow around stem.

Pin Cherry

Shrubby tree. Smooth, reddish bark, grows scaly and gray with age. Shiny green leaves are $2^1/_2$ - $4^1/_2$ in. long, thin and lance-shaped, with finely toothed edges. White flowers grow to tiny, bitter cherries.

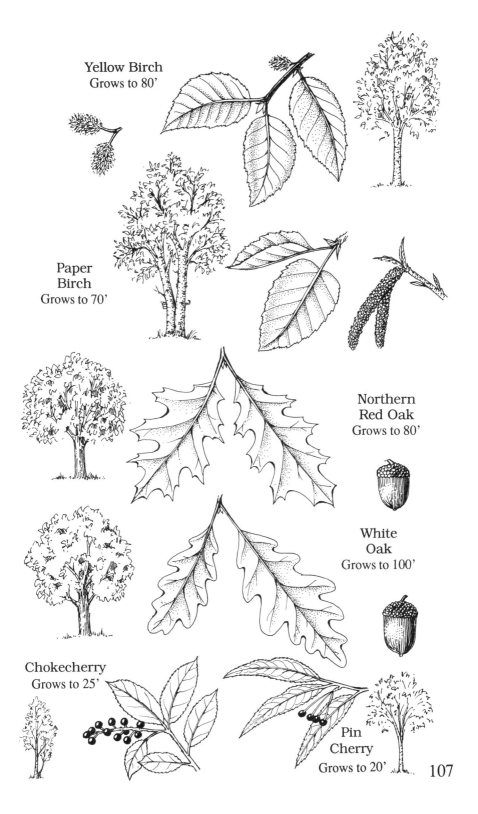

Yellow Birch
Grows to 80'

Paper Birch
Grows to 70'

Northern Red Oak
Grows to 80'

White Oak
Grows to 100'

Chokecherry
Grows to 25'

Pin Cherry
Grows to 20'

107

Shagbark Hickory

Bark is gray and peels off in long, shaggy strips. Pinnately compound leaves are 8 - 14 in. with toothed, pointed, hairy leaflets. Flowers are catkins. Fruits are round nuts inside ribbed husk.

Beech

Bark is gray, smooth with blotches. Leaves are $2\frac{1}{2}$ - 5 in. long, narrow, pointed and toothed ellipses. Yellow-green flowers hang in clusters. Fruit is two nuts inside a prickly husk.

Sycamore

Bark is smooth with patches of dark, flaking bark. Leaves are large, 4 - 8 in. with 3 - 5 pointed lobes and wavy, toothed edges. Fruits are 1 in., rough, green balls that hang on a stem.

Basswood (Linden)

Bark is gray and smooth, growing ridges with age. Leaves are large, round, toothed with a pointed end. Flowers are clusters that hang from a long, leaf-like stalk and grow to cluster of small, hairy, nut-like balls.

Butternut

Bark is smooth and gray developing rough ridges with age. Pinnately compound leaves are 15 - 30 in. long with lance-shaped, pointed, toothed leaflets. Catkin flowers turn to 2 in. oval nuts hanging in clusters.

Hophornbeam (Ironwood)

Bark is light brown with long, scaly ridges. Leaves are 2 - 5 in., yellow-green, pointed ellipses with toothed edges. Drooping, greenish flowers turn to clusters of bladder-like, papery seed pods.

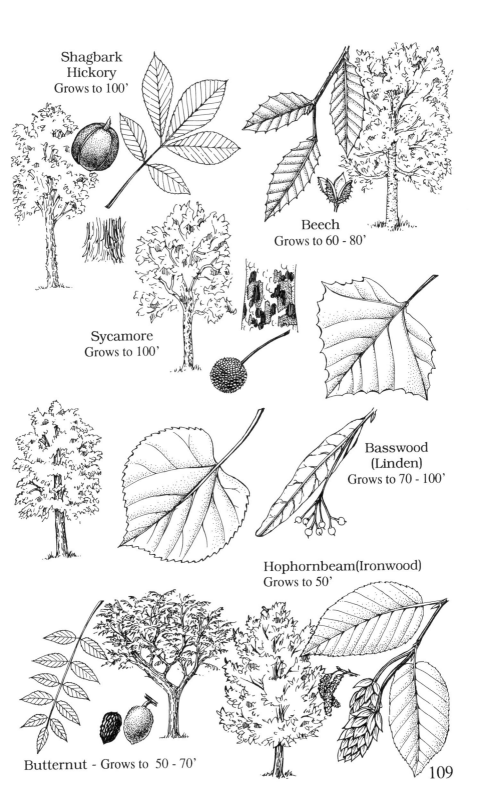

Shagbark
Hickory
Grows to 100'

Beech
Grows to 60 - 80'

Sycamore
Grows to 100'

Basswood
(Linden)
Grows to 70 - 100'

Hophornbeam(Ironwood)
Grows to 50'

Butternut - Grows to 50 - 70'

109

Hornbeam

Bark is smooth, gray. Shrubby tree with birch-like leaves. Drooping catkins turn to green clusters of 3-pointed leaf-like nutlets on stalks.

Coniferous Trees

Black Spruce

Bark is gray-black and scaly. Needles are blue-green, stiff, 4-sided, $^1/_2$ in. long and spiral all around drooping twigs. Cones are $^1/_2$ - 1 in. ovals and hang down. Grows in wet soils.

Red Spruce

Bark is red-brown and scaly. Needles are shiny green with lighter lines, 4-sided, $^1/_2$" long and spiral around twigs. Cones are 1 - 1$^1/_2$" long, cylinder shaped. Grows in wet areas.

White Spruce

Bark is gray-brown, smooth to scaly. Needles are blue-green with lighter lines, stiff, 4-sided, $^1/_2 - ^3/_4$", growing mostly on upper side of twig. Grows in coniferous forests, often in pure stands. Crushed needles emit skunk-like odor.

Balsam Fir

Bark is smooth with sap bubbles, becoming scaly with age. Needles are flat, shiny, dark green above with white stripes below, $^1/_2$ - 1." Cones are upright, 3 in., cylinder shaped, green-purple. Found in coniferous forests often in pure stands.

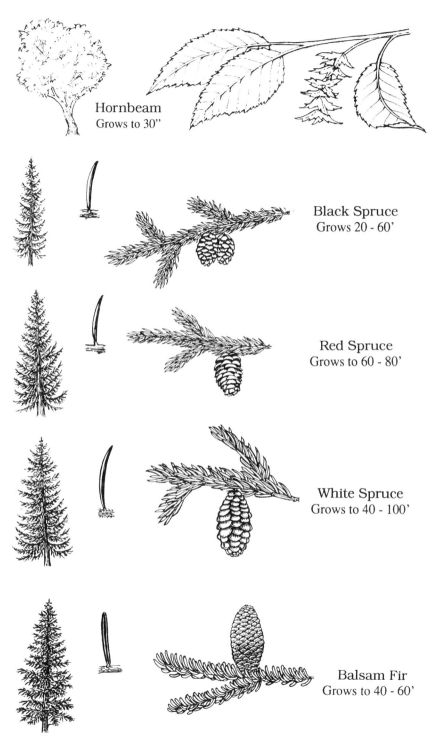

Hornbeam
Grows to 30"

Black Spruce
Grows 20 - 60'

Red Spruce
Grows to 60 - 80'

White Spruce
Grows to 40 - 100'

Balsam Fir
Grows to 40 - 60'

Eastern White Pine

Bark is gray and smooth, becoming brown and growing scaly ridges with age. Needles are blue-green, $2\frac{1}{2}$ - 5," clustered in groups of 5. Cones are 4 - 8" long, thin cylinders with long stalks.

Red Pine

Bark is red-brown with thick, scaly plates. Needles are dark green, 4 - 6 in., clusters of 2. Cones are 1 - $2\frac{1}{2}$" ovals.

Eastern Red Cedar

Bark is red-brown, fibrous and shredding. Leaves are flat, scaly, green branchlets. They are prickly to the touch. Fruit is dark blue berry.

Northern White Cedar

Bark is red-brown with fibrous, shredding ridges. Leaves are flat, overlapping, yellow-green scales. Cones are upright $\frac{1}{2}$" ovals. Grows in wet soil.

Eastern Hemlock

Bark is red-brown with deep ridges. Needles are flat, shiny, dark green above with two white stripes below, $\frac{1}{2}$". Cones are brown, oval, $\frac{1}{2}$" long and hang down on drooping branches.

Tamarack

Bark is red-brown with rounded scales. Needles are soft, blue-green, $\frac{1}{2}$", grow in clusters on twig spur. Needles turn yellow and are shed in the fall. Cones are $\frac{1}{2}$" ovals and sit upright. Grows best in wet soils.

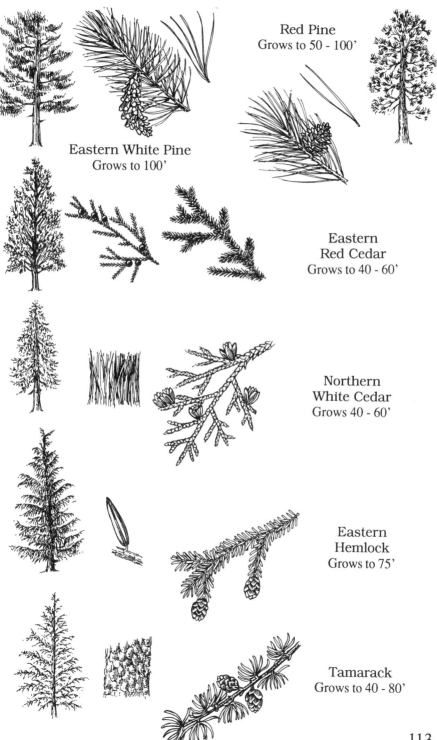

Red Pine
Grows to 50 - 100'

Eastern White Pine
Grows to 100'

Eastern
Red Cedar
Grows to 40 - 60'

Northern
White Cedar
Grows 40 - 60'

Eastern
Hemlock
Grows to 75'

Tamarack
Grows to 40 - 80'

113

Species Index
Birds

☐ bittern (American) 14

☐ blackbird (red-winged) 16

☐ bluebird (eastern) 20

☐ blue jay 26

☐ blue-winged teal 16

☐ bobolink 22

☐ Canadian goose 14

☐ cardinal 18

☐ catbird 32

☐ cedar waxwing 22

☐ chickadee 28

☐ cowbird (brown-headed) 34

☐ crossbill (red) 18

☐ crow 12

☐ finch (purple) 18

☐ flicker (northern) 26

flycatchers:

☐ *great crested flycatcher* 30

☐ *olive-sided flycatcher* 30

☐ goldfinch 20

☐ grackle (common) 34

☐ grosbeak (evening) 18

☐ grosbeak (rose-breasted) 18

grouse:

☐ *ruffed grouse* 12

☐ *spruce grouse* 12

hawks:

☐ *broad-winged hawk* 36

☐ *marsh hawk* 38

☐ *red-tailed hawk* 38

☐ *sharp-shinned hawk* 36

☐ heron (great blue) 16

☐ horned lark 22

☐ hummingbird (ruby-throated) 24

☐ junco (dark-eyed) 28

☐ kestrel 38

☐ killdeer 34

☐ kingbird (eastern) 30

☐ kingfisher (belted) 16

kinglets:

☐ *golden crowned kinglet* 24

☐ *ruby crowned kinglet* 24

☐ loon (common) 14

☐ mallard 16

☐ meadowlark 22

☐ merganser (common) 14

☐ mourning dove 34

☐ night hawk 12

nuthatches:

☐ *red breasted nuthatch* 24

☐ *white breasted nuthatch* 24

☐ oriole (northern) 22

☐ osprey 14

owls:

☐ *barred owl* 36

- ☐ *great horned owl* 36
- ☐ *saw-whet owl (northern)* 36
- ☐ *screech owl* 36
- ☐ phoebe (eastern) 30
- ☐ pine sisken 20
- ☐ redpoll (common) 18
- ☐ redstart 20
- ☐ robin 32
- ☐ rufous-sided towee 22
- ☐ shrike (northern) 38
- ☐ snipe 34
  sparrows:
- ☐ *fox sparrow* 28
- ☐ *house sparrow* 28
- ☐ *white-throated sparrow* 28
  swallows:
- ☐ *barn swallow* 20
- ☐ *tree swallow* 20
- ☐ *purple martin* 20
- ☐ thrasher (brown) 32
  thrushes:
- ☐ *hermit thrush* 32
- ☐ *wood thrush* 32
- ☐ tufted titmouse 24
- ☐ turkey (wild) 12
- ☐ veery 32
- ☐ vireo (red-eyed) 30
- ☐ vulture (turkey) 38
- ☐ woodcock 34

- ☐ wood duck 16
- ☐ whippoorwill 12
  woodpeckers:
- ☐ *downy woodpecker* 26
- ☐ *hairy woodpecker* 26
- ☐ *pileated woodpecker* 26
- ☐ *red headed woodpecker* 26
- ☐ *yellow-bellied sapsucker* 26
- ☐ wood pewee 30
- ☐ wren (house) 28
- ☐ yellowthroat 20

Wildflowers

- ☐ aster (New England) 48
- ☐ baneberry (white) 56
- ☐ bladder campion 58
- ☐ blue bead lily (yellow clintonia) 42
- ☐ blue-eyed grass 50
- ☐ blue flag 46
- ☐ bluets 50
- ☐ bunchberry 42
- ☐ chicory 48
- ☐ colt's foot 54
- ☐ columbine 52
- ☐ creeping bellflower 50
- ☐ evening primrose (common) 54
- ☐ fireweed 52
- ☐ fleabane (common) 58
- ☐ foam flower 58

- ☐ gentian (blind) 50
- ☐ ginger (wild) 44
- ☐ goldthread 42
- ☐ harebell 48
- ☐ hobblebush 56
- ☐ Indian pipe 42
- ☐ jack-in-the-pulpit 46
- ☐ lady slipper (pink) 44
- ☐ laurel (sheep) 52
- ☐ loosestrife (purple) 48
- ☐ marsh marigold (cowslip) 58
- ☐ mayflower (Canada) 56
- ☐ meadow rue (tall) 56
- ☐ meadowsweet 50
- ☐ milkweed (common) 52
- ☐ mullein (common) 54
- ☐ pearly everlasting 58
- ☐ pickerelweed 46
- ☐ pitcher plant (northern) 46
- ☐ Queen Anne's lace 56
- ☐ sarsaparilla 58

Solomon's seals:

- ☐ *false Solomon's seal* 42
- ☐ *great Solomon's seal* 42
- ☐ speedwell (common) 50
- ☐ spring beauty 44
- ☐ steeplebush 52
- ☐ St. Johnswort 54

trilliums:

- ☐ *painted trillium* 44
- ☐ *red trillium* 44
- ☐ trout lily 54
- ☐ vetch (cow) 48

violets:

- ☐ *common blue violet* 46
- ☐ *marsh blue violet* 46
- ☐ wood sorrel (common) 44
- ☐ yarrow 58

Mammals

bats:

- ☐ *hoary bat* 74
- ☐ *little brown bat* 74
- ☐ bear (black) 62
- ☐ beaver 70
- ☐ bobcat 62
- ☐ chipmunk (eastern) 72
- ☐ cottontail (eastern) 70
- ☐ coyote 64
- ☐ deer (white-tailed) 62
- ☐ fisher 64

foxes:

- ☐ *gray fox* 64
- ☐ *red fox* 64
- ☐ hare (snowshoe) 70
- ☐ lynx 62
- ☐ marten 64
- ☐ mink 66

☐ moose 62

moles:

☐ *hairy-tailed mole* 68

☐ *star-nosed mole* 68

mice:

☐ *deer mouse* 74

☐ *white-footed mouse* 74

☐ muskrat 70

☐ otter (river) 66

☐ porcupine 72

☐ raccoon 64

shrews:

☐ *long-tailed shrew* 68

☐ *short-tailed shrew* 68

☐ skunk (striped) 66

squirrels:

☐ *eastern gray squirrel* 72

☐ *northern flying squirrel* 72

☐ *red squirrel* 72

voles:

☐ *meadow vole* 74

☐ *woodland vole* 74

weasel:

☐ *long-tailed weasel* 66

☐ *short-tailed weasel (ermine)* 66

☐ woodchuck 70

Insects

☐ backswimmer 82

beetles:

☐ *ground beetle* 80

☐ *ladybird beetle* 80

☐ *whirligig beetle* 82

☐ bumble bee 78

butterflies:

☐ *admiral butterfly (red)* 88

☐ *admiral butterfly (white)* 88

☐ *checkerspot butterfly (silvery)* 90

☐ *eastern tailed blue butterfly* 90

☐ *fritillary butterfly (meadow)* 90

☐ *monarch butterfly* 88

☐ *mourning cloak butterfly* 88

☐ *painted lady butterfly* 90

☐ *pearly crescentspot butterfly* 90

☐ *sulfur butterfly (common)* 90

☐ *swallowtail butterfly (black)* 86

☐ *swallowtail butterfly (tiger)* 86

☐ *swallowtail butterfly (spicebush)* 86

☐ *viceroy butterfly* 88

☐ caterpillar (tent) 80

☐ cricket (field) 78

☐ daddy long legs 80

☐ damselfly 86

☐ dobsonfly 82

☐ dragonflies:

☐ *brown darner dragonfly* 84

☐ *Eliza skimmer dragonfly* 84

☐ *green darner dragonfly* 84

- [ ] *swift long-winged skimmer* 84
- [ ] *twelve-spot skimmer* 84
- [ ] firefly 78
- [ ] grasshopper 78
- [ ] katydid 78
- [ ] luna moth 86
- [ ] mayfly 84
- [ ] preying mantis 80
- [ ] walking stick 80
- [ ] water boatman 82
- [ ] water bug (giant) 82
- [ ] water strider 82
- [ ] yellow jacket 78

Amphibians

frogs:

- [ ] *bullfrog* 92
- [ ] *gray tree frog* 94
- [ ] *green frog* 94
- [ ] *pickerel frog* 92
- [ ] *spring peeper* 94
- [ ] *wood frog* 94
- [ ] red eft (newt) 92

salamanders:

- [ ] *dusky salamander* 92
- [ ] *spotted salamander* 92
- [ ] *two-lined salamander* 92
- [ ] toad (American) 94

Reptiles

snakes:

- [ ] *brown snake* 96
- [ ] *garter snake* 96
- [ ] *milk snake* 96
- [ ] *ribbon (eastern) snake* 96
- [ ] skink (five-lined) 98

turtles:

- [ ] *box (eastern) turtle* 98
- [ ] *painted turtle* 98
- [ ] *snapping turtle* 98
- [ ] *wood turtle* 98

Trees

- [ ] ash (white) 102

aspens:

- [ ] *bigtooth aspen* 104
- [ ] *quaking aspen* 104
- [ ] basswood (linden) 108
- [ ] balsam poplar 104
- [ ] beech 108

birches:

- [ ] *paper birch* 106
- [ ] *yellow birch* 106
- [ ] butternut 108

cedars:

- [ ] *eastern red cedar* 112
- [ ] *northern white cedar* 112
- [ ] chokecherry 106

- ☐ cottonwood (eastern) 104
- ☐ cherry (pin) 106
- ☐ elm 102
- ☐ fir (balsam) 110
- ☐ hemlock (eastern) 112
- ☐ hickory (shagbark) 108
- ☐ hophornbeam 108
- ☐ hornbeam 110

  maples:
- ☐ *red maple* 102
- ☐ *striped maple* 102
- ☐ *sugar maple* 102
- ☐ mountain ash 102

  oaks:
- ☐ *northern red oak* 106
- ☐ *white oak* 106

  pines:
- ☐ *red pine* 112
- ☐ *white (eastern) pine* 112

  spruces:
- ☐ *black spruce* 110
- ☐ *red spruce* 110
- ☐ *white spruce* 110
- ☐ sycamore 108
- ☐ tamarack 112

About the Author

Sheri Amsel has been writing and illustrating books and magazines for more than ten years. Her love of natural history began when she was a teenager in Vermont and grew into a strong interest in environmental science. This led to degrees in botany and zoology from the University of Montana and a master's degree in anatomy and biomedical illustration from Colorado State University.

During her early years in Vermont, she says, "I became attached to the idea that I could learn the names of every plant that I saw. I thought it might be wise to know how to survive on wild edibles or heal with medicinal plants. So I memorized wild herbal preparations. Many strange boiled meals occurred as a result of that early research.

"I still don't know why rubbing wild dock seeds on nettle burns sometimes works and whether chopped mullein leaves sprinkled on a fishing hole really will sedate the fish into being caught. But I grew up with the sense that learning such things had greatly enriched my life."

Sheri now lives with her husband and two sons in New York's Adirondack Mountains where she is an adjunct faculty member for the biology department at Plattsburgh State University and works on books, articles and educational programs from her home studio.